BECAUSE THESE THINGS
MATTER
A COMPILATION OF CULTURAL COMMENTARIES

TIM WILDMON

PRINTED IN THE UNITED STATES OF AMERICA

Printed by Signature Book Printing
8041 Cessna Ave, Ste 132
Gaithersburg, MD 20879

ISBN 9781935932574

American Family Association
107 Parkgate Drive
Tupelo, MS 38801
www.afa.net

Cover design by Maidie Jackson

Editorial contributions by Jennifer Nanney

Layout by
Darlene Swanson of Van-garde Imagery, Inc.

Project oversight by
Ed Vitagliano
Angie May

TABLE OF CONTENTS

Table of Contents

IN HIS STEPS

May 1995 – I traveled recently on a 10-day trip to Greece and Israel with a group led by my dad. Many people don't know that Dad used to lead trips to the Holy Land twice a year before he started American Family Association. This was his 19th tour.

It was a great trip, as the Bible came to life. We toured Athens and Corinth. We went to Mount Carmel, Nazareth, and the Jordan River. We took a boat ride on the Sea of Galilee. We saw where Jesus preached the Sermon on the Mount and where He fed the five thousand. We then went on to Jericho and up to Jerusalem, where we spent four nights.

We went to Bethlehem before going to the Garden of Gethsemane, Calvary, and the Garden Tomb. We saw the Mount of Olives, the Temple Mount, the Dead Sea, and many, many other sights – too many to mention in this column.

Indeed, it is one thing to read stories from the Scriptures, but it's another to literally walk where Jesus walked. And I do mean *literally*. In Jerusalem we followed the exact route Jesus walked the night of his betrayal when He was led to appear before the religious leaders.

Many places we visited were interesting from a historical perspective. But some places, for the sinner saved by grace, caused tears to well up and a lump in the throat. For me, one of those places was the Church of the Beatitudes overlooking the Sea of Galilee. I was the last tourist to return to the bus. To look out over the grassy field by the water and imagine Jesus surrounded by all those people who loved Him and whom He loved was an awesome experience. I thought about those who had gathered with the Lord, those whom He had healed from sickness and disease. Jesus Christ, the Son of God, lived and taught some 2,000 years ago in the very place I was standing. He taught:

> *"Blessed are the poor in spirit, for theirs is the kingdom of heaven.*
>
> *"Blessed are those who mourn, for they shall be comforted.*
>
> *"Blessed are the gentle, for they shall inherit the earth.*
>
> *"Blessed are those who hunger and thirst for righteousness, for they shall be satisfied.*
>
> *"Blessed are the merciful, for they shall receive mercy.*
>
> *"Blessed are the pure in heart, for they shall see God.*
>
> *"Blessed are the peacemakers, for they shall be called sons of God.*
>
> *"Blessed are those who have been persecuted for the sake of righteousness, for theirs is the kingdom of heaven.*

"Blessed are you when people insult you and persecute you, and falsely say all kinds of evil against you because of Me. Rejoice and be glad, for your reward in heaven is great; for in the same way they persecuted the prophets who were before you."

– Matthew 5:3-12

If you are a fellow Christian pilgrim, I hope you too can one day journey across the Atlantic and visit the Holy Land.

DIRECTION MAKES A DIFFERENCE

June 1995 – Ever since I can remember, I have been a sports fanatic. I've loved playing and watching football, basketball, and baseball since I was a kid. The older I get, the more I enjoy watching and the less I enjoy playing – or so says my body.

When I was 8 years old, I used to carry around a transistor radio and listen to the St. Louis Cardinals all summer. I knew everything about the Cardinals: batting averages, ERAs, Lou Brock's number of stolen bases – you name it. Baseball, bike-riding around the neighborhood, swimming, and the Cardinals on radio – that was my life in the summer of 1971.

It was about that time my dad began taking me to Mississippi State football games. I became a loyal fan of the Bulldogs. It was then I learned of humility (and humiliation) every time MSU played the legendary Alabama teams of Coach Bear Bryant. Sports has always been a big part of my life. In fact, to this day, the first part of the newspaper I read each morning is the sports section.

I'll be the first to admit that, from time to time, I have gotten this love for sports a little out of perspective – for instance, talking Alison into going to St. Louis for our honeymoon. Now hold on there, ladies; it's not what you might think. I mean, sure we took in three Cardinals games, but we also went to Six Flags, the Arch, and Grant's Farm. (And it doesn't get much more romantic than going down the "Screaming Eagle" hand in hand.)

Now it's 1995, and my oldest son, Wesley, is 5, and he has begun to show some interest in sports. Soccer, however, just wasn't his bag. So I decided to let him try T-ball, and I would take my coaching skills from church-league softball (no victories in three years) onto the T-ball field. (For the record, I never had any material to work with in church league softball. My guys – the laughingstock of the league – were the Bad News Bears, 20 years later. On a "good" day, our team was very, very bad. Otherwise, we were absolutely pitiful and completely inept.)

Ever since I had told Wesley I was going to coach, he kept asking me – about every other day – when we were going to start.

"Soon, son," I would tell him.

"Does that mean tomorrow, the day after tomorrow, or the day after that?" he would ask. (This was several weeks before our first practice.)

Finally, our first practice arrived on a Saturday morning in late April.

Now, keep in mind here, these 12 kids (5- and 6-year-olds) I had drafted had never had any experience in organized baseball before. I didn't know but three or four of them, they didn't know me, and most of them didn't know each other. I sat down on third base and told them to gather around. Everyone got a piece of gum, we had a short prayer, and we started talking baseball.

We talked and then we practiced – if you can call it that – for about an hour.

One field over was another team coached by a friend of mine. It was probably their third or fourth practice. On our water break, he challenged me – in front of my players – to a short game.

"Yeah, Coach, let's play them!" a few of my players said to me.

What was I supposed to say? "No, kids, we're going to work on the fundamentals," would seem like I was ducking the challenge. It also sounded boring. I remember when I was a kid, I wanted to play, not practice. So I decided to take a step on the wild side and play after practicing for just one hour. So we took our gear next door, and I explained to my team what "on deck" meant, not to sling their bat, and to listen to their base coach.

I thought to myself, *Oh, well … you learn by doing.*

My first two batters did OK. They hit the ball and ran to first base. *This is going pretty well,* I thought.

Then my third batter came to the plate. The little guy took a good whack, hit the ball, and began to run his heart out. He was fast, too. He was "diggin' it," as we say in baseball circles. My little man was runnin' hard. There was only one problem. You guessed it. The lil' fellow was running to *third* base – not first.

As you can imagine, the adults – including the little fellow's dad – were bending over in laughter. I couldn't help myself either. I told the other coach that my guy meant to do that just to throw *his* team off. The other team – having practiced more than we – were all laughing as well. However, I knew I had a long way to go when I looked over at my dugout and saw my little girls and boys yelling for their teammate to keep running to the next base – wherever it was!

The dad went over, bent down and put his arm around his son, and told him what he did wrong and what to do next time – all the while trying to hold back his own laughter.

The basics. The fundamentals. The rules of the game. In the Christian life, we often spend a lot of energy "blowin' and goin'" in the wrong direction, don't we? And we do this, many times with the best of intentions, when what we really need to do is stop and listen to the Master teacher through the reading of His word and through prayer. I've been really convicted recently of the importance of those two things. I have asked the Lord for a new hunger for prayer and daily devotional time so that I may know His direction for my life, both generally and day to day. The Lord says if we will seek Him, we will find Him. But how much time do we spend seeking? More time than we spend reading the sports page, I hope. Ouch!

It's going to be an interesting two months of T-ball ahead. It's going to be fun. And, oh yes, the name I chose for our team? The Cardinals, of course … what else?

WHY DO YOU DO IT?

August 1995 – "Why do you do this?" is the question I have been asked many times by reporters and others, concerning our work here at American Family Association. Some ask this question in the "What right do you have to force your morals down my throat?" vein. Others – sometimes fellow Christians – ask this question in a "You don't really expect to change anything, do you?" sort of way.

When I began working at AFA in 1986, I was quick to take offense at questions like this. If I was on the phone, I would snap back fairly quickly. Now, after nearly 10 years under this roof, I rarely get offended anymore. In 1986 I would read something negative in the newspaper about Dad or AFA, and it would bother me greatly for days, sometimes weeks. Now, I just yawn and turn the page.

Why do I do what I do here at AFA? Well, life goes by quickly here on Earth. The only real legacy we leave is our children. What kind of country am I going to leave to my children and grandchildren? Do I have a responsibility to them beyond food, clothing, shelter, and education? Yes, I believe strongly that I do.

I believe the United States of America is the greatest country on the face of the earth and is worth preserving. But it doesn't take a rocket scientist (I've never really met a rocket scientist, but I'm sure they are smart people) to see our country is in a moral mess. Drugs, crime, divorce, violence, disrespect for authority, abortion, sexually transmitted diseases, and on and on we could go.

Yes, we've always had social/cultural/moral problems. But never ever have we had so many that run so deep that are tearing at the very fabric that separates civilization from barbarism. And modern technology has nothing to do with the type of civility and barbarism I'm writing about here. As Charles Colson writes in his book *Against the Night*: "The barbarians of the new dark age are pleasant and articulate men and women. They carry briefcases, not spears. But their assault on culture is every bit as devastating as the barbarian invasion of Rome."

So why do we do what we do here at AFA? Because we love God and want to honor Him by taking a stand for biblical righteousness (see Matt. 5:10). Because we love America and don't want to see her destroyed by the cancer of moral decline. And because we love our children and want to give them a country with some semblance of civility and morality, so that they, too, can enjoy all that is great about America.

KEYS TO MAKING A DIFFERENCE: UNDERSTANDING, WISDOM, AND INVOLVEMENT

October 1995 – When I was a kid, my dad used to order season tickets to Mississippi State football games. They would arrive in the mail sometime in the late summer, and he would show them to me. I would look at them and hold them, counting down the days until we would load up the car and drive to Jackson or Starkville to watch the Bulldogs play. Those cool, crisp, Saturday afternoons in October and November of yesteryear are fond memories. I'll never forget them.

Now, years later, Dad doesn't go to games much anymore; he listens to them on the radio or watches them on television. But I still go, and now I take my oldest son, Wesley, who is 6. I have taken Wesley from time to time the last couple of years, but he has never really had any interest in the games (basketball or football). I had a tough time figuring this out. I just thought it was genetic or something that my son would enjoy sporting events the way I did. But it has been hard to get him to go with me, and he hasn't shared my enthusiasm for the games. Usually, a few minutes into the game, he asks when we're going home. (I certainly attribute some of this to his youth, and he may well be burned out, given the fact that he attended his first college football game when he was not quite 5 months old.)

Well, I talked him into going to the first game of the season – September 2, just Wesley and me. We got to the stadium, and the pregame festivities were enough to hold his attention. *This is great,* I thought. *Wesley is finally starting to enjoy coming with me.*

Then sure enough, after about a quarter, he began the "When are we going home?" questions.

I answered him once or twice with the standard "It will be over in a lil' while; do you want a Coke?" line.

But after a couple of delay-tactic answers, something new came to my mind. A profound thought it was.

You know, Tim, I thought to myself, *Wesley doesn't understand what's going on down there on the field. All he sees is 'a bunch of people in uniforms running wildly around on a painted field with a ball, hitting each other, stopping occasionally to separate because some guys dressed like zebras run around blowing whistles and waving their arms. And as for the people in the stands, including my dad, they make loud noises, clap their hands, and yell things at the people on the field who can't hear a word they are saying because everyone is trying to talk – or yell – at once.' That's football through Wesley's eyes,* I thought. *I would want to know when we were going home too if I were Wesley.*

In the words of Ricky Ricardo, I needed to do "a little 'splainin'" to Wesley.

"Do you know what's going on out there, Wesley?"

He shook his head no.

"Let me tell you," I said. "You see the Bulldogs in maroon, and you see the Tigers in blue? Well ..."

I took about 10 minutes and explained in as simple terms as possible (which is not hard for me) the object of the game, the meaning and purpose for the actions. I pointed out the scoreboard, the clock, and how to score points. I taught him as the action went along. He didn't grasp everything, by any means, but he did begin to watch the action and ask questions of me. He was now somewhat interested in the game. He didn't ask again when we were going home.

The Holy Scriptures say a lot about understanding and wisdom ... about insight and knowledge. In 1 Chronicles 12:23-37, we find the story of the different groups of men who were to fight with David against the Philistines, and the different strengths each group possessed. One group was called "*the sons of Issachar, men who understood the times, with knowledge of what Israel should do*" (v. 32).

If we are Christians, we need to ask God to open our eyes so that we may know what to do in 1995 America to defend our families, Christian values, and Christian principles against the popular culture. We must be on the field, not on the sidelines.

If we ask God for understanding, He will give it to us. The Bible says there is a great spiritual war going on between the forces of good (God) and evil (Satan). If we believe this – if our eyes have been opened – then what are we doing for our side?

Are we praying for America and our leaders? Are we voting for men and women of character and conviction? Are we supporting – through prayer and, when possible, financial support – groups like American Family Association and others standing up for moral values? Are we writing letters or making phone calls on a moral issue? How about volunteering time at the local crisis pregnancy center?

None of us can do it all. But let me encourage you to pray and do what you can to make our country a better place to live and raise a family. And pray daily for understanding and wisdom. You'll find out, as Wesley did, that things will be a whole lot more interesting and meaningful.

And, oh yes, for those who are wondering … State won the game.

PRECIOUS MEMORIES: CELEBRATING A LEGACY OF FAITH AND FAMILY

November-December 1995 – There is no other time of year when we think more about our families than the Thanksgiving/ Christmas season. We purchase gifts, we cook food, we travel long distances, we mail cards and letters, etc., etc. All for our families. This time of year, we even hug the necks of the ones that get on our nerves. (Not that any of my family members get on my nerves, you know.) Yes, Thanksgiving and Christmas are about the goodness and blessings of our Lord first and foremost; but then they're about families gathering together to celebrate that goodness.

Remember the old song that said, "Over the river and through the woods to Grandmother's house we go"? Well, for 32 years, that's exactly what I did on those two holidays.

My mom was raised by Bill and Eloise Bennett way out in the country in the northeast corner of Mississippi Hill Country. Cotton and soybean country. And that's where my grandparents lived until earlier this year, when my ailing grandaddy had to be

15

moved into a nursing home here in Tupelo. He passed away a couple of months later. My grandmother, who had moved with him, lives in a seniors' home here. And for the first time in 32 years, I won't be getting in a car – either as passenger in one of my parents' many station wagons or as a driver with my own kids – and going to the old house in the country for the holidays. I miss it already.

Ironically, my dad's dad, PaPa (that's "Paw Paw" in the South), 91, also passed away over the summer. So it's been a year of great loss in our family. But I thank the Lord I was able to know my two grandfathers for 32 years. I have treasured memories that I will take with me the rest of my life and pass down to my three children.

I am a very nostalgic person. I enjoy talking about memories with my family and friends. Thank God for memories. This year I especially remember Christmas past. If you would permit me a little self-indulgence here, I would like to pay tribute to my two grandads in this column.

We still have the eight-millimeter black-and-white films – no sound, of course – of my grandaddy walking the Shetland pony around the front yard of that old country home with his first grandson, Timmy, on the back of the pony. Christmas 1966. He bought that pony, my mom told me recently, just for the seven or eight times a year his grandchildren would come to the farm. I don't know what ever happened to that pony. I think he sold it when we got too big to ride.

Grandaddy Bennett was a farmer for most of his life. The first and last time I ever fed farm animals was back when I would spend a few days on his farm. Those were also the first and last times I was awakened by a rooster. My Grandaddy Bennett was a very hard worker and often worked two jobs – the farm and the factory – to support his family of six. One of my fondest memories was when all the grandchildren would get in line so that Grandaddy could "count our ribs." He enjoyed seeing us all laugh and have a good time.

Grandaddy Bennett was a faithful member of Red Bud Baptist Church for as long as I can remember. The little country church seats about 50 and is where Grandmother and Grandaddy celebrated their 50th wedding anniversary just a few years back. I videotaped it.

Needless to say, I have a lot of fond memories of my Grandfather Bennett. He was, in many ways, a Christian example for me and his entire family. I loved him very much, and he will be missed greatly this holiday season.

My PaPa Wildmon raised his family about 40 miles away in Tippah County during the Great Depression and World War II. There's a line in "Song of the South" (by the country band Alabama) that says, "Somebody told us Wall Street fell / We were so poor we couldn't tell." That was my PaPa Wildmon's world, my dad tells me – but it was not unlike almost everyone else in the rural South during those years.

PaPa told me all about those times. I've got all those memories packed away. From the first time an automobile came down the dirt road till the first and only time (as far as I know) PaPa flew in an airplane. For years my dad led tours to the Holy Land, and he would, from time to time, ask PaPa to go with him.

"No, thank you," he would say. "Tippah County's holy land to me."

He didn't care for travel and always wanted to go home – wherever he was – long before my MaMa was ready to go.

"Would you just sit down and wait a little?" she would say.

They were married 67 years. I remember their 50th anniversary celebration at the First United Methodist Church in Ripley. MaMa Wildmon passed away three years ago, and PaPa never was the same. I'm sure they're happy now.

Well, I could go on and on. PaPa Wildmon raised a pretty good son, wouldn't you say? In fact, he raised three boys and two girls, but of course I'm partial to one.

Precious memories about two fine Christian men who influenced my life forever.

Have a wonderful holiday season – and be sure to pack those memories away with that shirt Aunt Sue gives you.

"Honey, do you think Aunt Sue would ever know if I took this back and exchanged it for …"

GOD'S MESSAGE CAN BE HARD TO SWALLOW

January 1996 – Can you imagine being inside the belly of a whale? Honestly, I don't want to imagine being inside the belly of a whale – or "huge fish," as the New International Version reads – but such was the situation of a man named Jonah. His story is between the books of Obadiah and Micah.

The first few verses read:

> *The word of the Lord came to Jonah the son of Amittai saying, "Arise, go to Nineveh the great city and cry against it, for their wickedness has come up before Me." But Jonah rose up to flee to Tarshish from the presence of the Lord. So he went down to Joppa, found a ship which was going to Tarshish, paid the fare and went down into it to go with them to Tarshish from the presence of the Lord. – Jonah 1:1-3*

A few thoughts related – some not so closely – to this story.

Now, I don't know about you, but if I were going to run away from the Lord, I would find a more appealing place to go than a town called Tarshish. Sounds like something New Yorkers put on a hotdog.

I wonder what was going through Jonah's mind when he decided to "run away" from Almighty God. How does one make travel plans for such a mission? Somehow, I think Jonah knew he couldn't get away from the Lord. Maybe he thought that if he turned and went the other way, the Lord would accept his answer and drop the issue – or call someone else to go tell those folks they were wicked. Calling people to repentance from sin and wickedness was not the most enjoyable of tasks in those days. Men weren't waiting in line to go speak to the people about the holiness and righteousness of God and His judgment. The same is true today.

When I speak to churches and other groups, I usually tell them right off the bat that I'd rather be talking about love, peace, and happiness than about pornography, homosexuality, and moral decline. And I do try to balance my messages with the hope that only a personal relationship with Jesus Christ can bring. But these moral issues must be discussed and addressed. We can't just sit in our "bless-me clubs" while our country – morally speaking – goes to hell in a hand basket. Let's see ... how can I be more direct?

From time to time, we get letters from well-meaning Christians who say, "We just need to concentrate on leading people to faith in Christ, and the rest will take care of itself. You people get involved in too much controversy."

I'm sure that one of the reasons Jonah tried to run from God was that he didn't want to get involved in controversy. Who needs the criticism? Who needs the heat?

My response to my "Just preach love!" friends is the New Testament. Jesus didn't go looking for trouble and controversy, but He met it – in large part – because of what He stood for and stood against. His values. His standards. Yes, His morality. He stood *for* holiness and righteousness and *against* sin and wickedness. It seems to me it was when He spoke against sin that (in today's vernacular) ticked people off. The same can be said of Paul, Peter, and many of the other leaders in the early church.

People don't want to hear about sin or the consequences of sin. Many pastors have been run out of churches for preaching against sin.

Let me finish by saying it is wise to do what the Lord calls us to do, regardless of the unpopularity of the task. And besides, there are worse places to be than preaching in Nineveh.

Like the belly of a whale, for instance.

AN EGGSCELLENT QUESTION

August 1996 – Did the chicken come before the egg? Or did the egg come before the chicken? This is a question that has perplexed man down through the ages. Abraham Lincoln and Stephen Douglas went at this issue during one of their legendary debates, although you never read about it anywhere. The "egg first" crowd showed up for Douglas and the "chicken first" for Lincoln.

The vote was split evenly, so ultimately, other issues decided the presidential election of 1860. In a similar vein, in terms of what's more important, the Christian community often divides itself along these lines: One side says it's more important to evangelize – to change hearts – than to be socially active; the other side says it's more important to be socially active – to save America while we still can – than it is to evangelize.

It seems that most Christians fall somewhere in the middle here. In other words, it's a both/and situation rather than an either/or situation.

Jesus Christ gave us what is known as the Great Commission, which is a clear commandment for His followers to spread His message of repentance, forgiveness, mercy, and salvation to all peoples. Christians – if they want to be true to their Lord – have no choice but to reach others for Christ – to evangelize. It is of the utmost importance.

On the other hand, we have numerous passages instructing Christians to stand – in a paganistic or hostile public, if they must – for the ideals, the values, and the virtues that are expressed in the Scriptures ... to impact the culture around them *for* good, *for* righteousness, and *against* evil.

The Holy Bible is truth.

In the current political and social climate of America, those who stand for biblical morality, especially as it relates to homosexuality, are the ones called "hatemongers." Righteousness is turned on its head, and we are made out to be the bad guys. We're intolerant, we're bigoted, and we're KKK types. End of argument. Often, in an attempt to really make us look foolish, we're told that Jesus was a man of mercy and not judgment.

But really, He was, is, and will be ... both.

For instance, in the case of the woman caught in adultery, while not condemning her, Jesus *did* pass judgment on her actions, telling her to "go and leave your life of sin." Yes, Jesus used the "s" word. Can you believe it? He called adultery "sin," but He extended love and mercy to the sinner. That is what Christians should be about. Call sinners to repentance, but never stop calling sin, sin. And sin is – after all – what separates man from God and why Jesus came in the first place – to reconcile a sinful man to a holy God.

Christians cannot hate anyone. Hate is just as much a sin as is adultery, stealing, or immoral behaviors, such as homosexuality. In fact, the consequences of hate are often worse for the individual and for society than are the consequences of other sins. The love of God, as expressed through Jesus, overcomes hatred.

So we must evangelize, and our Christian faith must be the basis for social action. Where God places you to reach others – or what avenue He gives you for expressing social justice – is individual, but all Christians should be concerned with both.

How's that for a down-the-middle answer? But I did give you an answer, which is more than some politicians (and even some preachers) give us when they split an answer down the middle.

So back to the chicken and the egg. I've always gone with the chicken on this one. I figure, God made the animals – including the bird every other animal tastes like – right out of thin air. Poof! Then the chicken began producing eggs. But you know, this is one I can bend on a little. I can hang out with the "egg first" crowd. I would never want to be considered narrow-minded, bigoted, or judgmental by the EFLETF lobby (Egg First Love and Equality Task Force).

GOD'S GOLD MEDALS

October 1996 – Like millions of Americans, I greatly enjoyed watching the Olympics this summer. And as much as I enjoyed our basketball "Dream Team" and the swimming, diving, and track-and-field events, it was those 80-pound ladies on the gym floor and balance beam that left me awestruck.

These young athletes often seemed to do things that defied gravity. The balance beam is only four inches in width, yet these girls would do up to three consecutive flips without using their hands to balance. Simply amazing.

However, with the exception of a few Olympic athletes, most are not in the national and international spotlight very often. Certainly, the gymnasts I mentioned are not well-known names like David Robinson of the United States basketball team or Carl Lewis of the United States track-and-field team. Yet they worked, toiled, and sweated for years – behind the scenes in some gym out of the limelight – for that moment of decision and a chance to win the gold medal.

These world class athletes wanted to represent their countries well and win the gold for their countrymen. In the same way, Christians should always be in training for the task God has called us to, whatever it may be. When we have that moment of decision, we don't want to fail the Lord.

Very few of us are going to be the David Robinsons of the Christian faith. Most of us are in life's obscure gym, working out where no one really sees us. Hour after hour, day after day, week after week doing those things that, if we are faithful, in the end will bring us a gold medal.

And just as David Robinson bowed his head and received a gold medal, so too did that unknown gymnast from Romania. Both were rewarded by the Olympic judges. Likewise will Christians be rewarded by our Lord Jesus Christ – the great judge – if we continue in faithfulness to serve and obey God. The importance the task holds in our own eyes, or in the eyes of the world, is of little consequence. Faithful service is the important thing.

BATTLE OVER BELLY BUTTON BLURS MESSAGE

February 1997 – For this month's topic, we shall begin with a question that has sent many a seminary student packing: Did Adam have a navel?

Before we attempt to answer this question, we need to cover a little background material. First, who was Adam? Adam, of course, was the first human created by Almighty God and also the first human being who tried to pass the buck. Later, President Harry Truman would make up for us guys with his famous, "The buck stops here" line, but Adam – he was ready for a nap, and he didn't like the tone in the Lord's voice, so he blamed Eve for his partaking of the forbidden fruit.

Now, as a general rule, what Adam did was perfectly normal and makes for a good marriage. Of course, I'm talking about do-ing – without question – whatever your wife tells you to do. I do this today, as do most of my friends, and we're cool with it. Adam did this, and – well, his problem is pretty well summed up in one verse in Genesis 3:6, which says, "*When the woman saw that the tree was good for food, and that it was a delight to the eyes, and that the tree was desirable to make one wise, she took from its fruit and ate; and she gave also to her husband with her, and he ate."*

Actually, Adam's problems began with just one sentence in one verse.

One minute you're enjoying paradise in the heavenly hammock, 75 degrees, sunshine splashing down as a gentle breeze plays on your face ... everything's great. Then your wife reaches over and says, "Here, Honey," and hands you a piece of fruit while you're not half paying attention – maybe even got your eyes closed – when you take a nice bite and WHAM! The next thing you know, you've changed the plight of the human race for eternity.

This was a bad day in the life of Adam.

But did Adam have a navel? That was our question.

Answer: Really, I don't know, and I don't care.

What I've used here, students, is an exaggerated example of the kind of "issue" or question that often takes up far too much of Christians' time and diverts attention from the things that matter most. This is also representative of the type of "issue" that often divides the Christian community so unnecessarily. In an even broader sense, the traditional values or pro-family movement sometimes divides along such trivial lines.

Just what are our goals and objectives? It seems to me they should include:

1. Reaching people with the Good News that Jesus Christ is the Son of God and the only way to peace and everlasting life.

2. Upholding the ten Commandments, the Sermon on the Mount, and biblical morality in an age of moral relativism.

With three young children now, I have a vested interest at heart. For my children and grandchildren, I want an America that honors the law of God again. Maybe I'm living in la-la land with this hope, but I know one thing: I'm going to fight for this dream until the day I die. I've staked my life on the Holy Bible being true and Jesus Christ being God.

America is spiritually sick. In fact, I'd say she's on life support. And those of us who are pursuing the two goals mentioned above have the medicine. We can help lead this great country we love to spiritual wellness and moral sanity. But we've got to decide what is important in life, and we've got to keep the main thing, the main thing. Too often we allow trivial matters or questions to divide us or get us off course when we need to keep a "foxhole" mentality.

Do you agree?

"Yes, but did Adam have a navel?" you ask.

Well, let me tell you one thing, buddy. In the first place, you haven't paid attention to one thing I've said, and secondly, any ignoramus knows it isn't a navel – it's a belly button. And another thing …

MESSAGE OF LIVING BY GOD'S WORD STILL RINGS TRUE

July 1997 – "You want to go with me?" Dad asked.

"Yeah! Can I?" I responded with childlike enthusiasm.

"Get your things together, and we'll be leaving in the morning."

The year was 1977, and my dad, Don Wildmon, had just left the pulpit of First United Methodist Church in Southaven, Mississippi, to form what was then known as the National Federation for Decency. Before his very eyes, he had witnessed a moral decline in America and felt called by the Lord to do something about it. So he founded National Federation for Decency (now American Family Association).

One of the primary ways to grow an organization is by getting in front of people and convincing them you have a cause worth supporting. So in 1977, that's what Dad did. Yes, he traveled by plane sometimes (when he could afford it or when an invitation included airfare), but most of the time – early on anyway – Dad got in his old green Buick and drove to his destination. Sometimes, when school wasn't in progress, he would invite me to go along. For a kid 14 years old, the idea of traveling to new parts of the country was very exciting. Also, I didn't like Dad traveling long distances alone. It had to be lonely being a one-man organization, I thought. And even at that age, I sensed that Dad needed some family support for his decision to leave the security of a nice church and blaze a trail into parts unknown.

So Mom helped me pack a few items, and off Dad and I went to Atlanta, Georgia. From Southaven, which is just across the Tennessee state line from Memphis, this was about an eight-hour trip. I often carried games I could play by myself when we went on these journeys. And Dad and I would talk about where we were going, what he would be doing, and finally about my favorite subjects – the St. Louis Cardinals and Mississippi State sports. He didn't follow the Cardinals religiously like I did, but he did know enough about the Bulldogs to talk for a while. Mostly he just listened to me. I also remember when some 1950s music would come on the radio, I would give him a strange look, and he would laugh and sometimes sing along. Then I would give him an even stranger look because, while Dad was a great preacher in my eyes, his singing left a whole lot to be desired. A whole lot. Still does. (Sorry, Dad.)

When we got to Atlanta, we found our host church. I can't remember what night of the week it was; I just know it was summertime in the Deep South, and it was very hot and humid. The church had about 150 people packed inside, and the doors were open in the back. It was also the first time I had ever been in a Pentecostal worship service with tambourines and all. I sat near the back as Dad delivered his message. Dad was very energetic behind the pulpit – as Methodists go anyway – and the shouts of "Amen!" and "Praise the Lord!" and (my personal favorite) "Come on!" did nothing but enhance his vigor. Dad, a lifelong Methodist, was right at home with our Pentecostal brothers and sisters. Me? The closest thing I had been exposed to that was anything like that worship service was at youth camp at Camp Lake Stephens – singing without hymnals, moving around, a little loud, hands lifted high. Why, this seemed like a … seemed like … a pep rally for a Mississippi State football game to me! *"Can they do this in church?"* I thought. *"Is this OK with God?"*

Looking back, I laugh about that night. Having been a Christian for many years now, I've found the saying true (I'm not sure who said it, but I believe it was the father of Methodism himself, John Wesley): "I would rather try and cool down a fanatic than try and warm up a corpse." These folks just loved Jesus, and they were excited about Him. What's wrong with that? Nothing.

But what struck me that night in 1977, as much as anything, was that these folks were connecting with Dad's message. His sadness for the moral decline in America was their sadness. His longing to try and do something about it was their longing. Dad said what the problems were and what – as he saw it in those days – the answers were. That if we were to have any hope for America, Christians – above all people – should rise up and be the salt and light Jesus says we should be in Matthew 5.

After the service, the church gave him an offering. Many people gave him their individual home addresses and said, "Send me your newsletter. I want to support you, Brother Wildmon." And so the ministry grew and gained influence. Who really knows, but perhaps you are reading this today because someone who was at that worship service in Atlanta supported us way back when.

We're still fighting. We're still moving ahead. We're still defending and promoting Christian principles. I see so much more we can do with your support and the Lord's leading in these coming years.

Nowadays, Dad and I rarely ride the highways together to far-off places so he can speak to groups. In fact, he doesn't travel or speak much anymore. After 20 years of beating that trail, one does tend to tire. But because of his early efforts, we now have supporters – many of whom are Pentecostal, I might add. Many are Methodist and Baptist. We have a lot of Catholic supporters, some Presbyterian, and others. The message for a better America, where morality and virtue still matter, still connects with hundreds of thousands of people of all different stripes.

Thank you for your support of AFA. Now, let's roll our sleeves up and get back to work.

THE GNATS ARE SWARMING
AROUND DUMBO

October 1997 – Do you ever wonder why there are so many Christian denominations? I do a little, although I don't spend a lot of time on it.

Jesus prayed that his followers would be one even as He and the Father are one. I'm not sure I understand the full meaning of that particular prayer, but I find it impossible to believe that, as long as human beings have independent thinking capabilities, there will ever be complete unity in the Christian church. And I don't think Jesus would have asked his Heavenly Father for us to do the impossible, so I've got to believe what Jesus meant, basically, was that Christians must have a spirit of love, charity, and grace – even when they have sincere and strongly held differences. My guess is, you have theological or doctrinal differences among good people in your own local church, whatever the denomination. I know that's the case in my church.

I was raised in the United Methodist Church but now attend an independent Evangelical church, and on matters of doctrine – although I have evolved and migrated somewhat – I am basically aligned with what the Southern Baptist Church believes. However, I have friends, colleagues, and family in a variety of different denominations, and when I talk with them, most are very articulate and convincing about why they believe the way they do. I like to pick their brains and see if they can defend what they confess. Almost every time, I'm surprised. One day I lean Presbyterian, and the next day I tilt charismatic. No, wait a minute … I like what the Episcopalians say about this and what John Wesley said about that. I remember talking over several doctrinal issues with a Catholic friend. I threw him a few Protestant hardballs, just knowing I'd have him stumped, since the Pope was nowhere around, and it was just him and me. I don't remember all the details, but I do remember thinking he had some very reasonable answers to my questions. He even cited several biblical references to back up his explanations.

I try to listen, learn, and understand whenever I talk about religion with others, even if they're not Christian. This doesn't threaten my faith in Jesus Christ, but it does serve to challenge my presuppositions and make me a better student of the Bible.

With all the different branches of the Christian tree – and I am certainly one who believes that doctrine is important and that we should all search and study the Holy Scriptures to know what is true and right – it really blesses my heart when I see Christians of different stripes working together on a common project in the name of our Lord Jesus Christ. Recently, Northeast Mississippi hosted a Franklin Graham crusade in my hometown. It was a great community effort and a wonderful evangelistic outreach.

On a national scale, I have been absolutely thrilled to see the many denominations and pro-family organizations coming together in one voice of moral objection to the mighty Disney Corporation. Disney, as has been well documented in the _AFA_ Journal for over three years now, is the leading American company pushing the homosexual social agenda, in addition to many other immoral and occultic products and practices.

This summer, the Southern Baptist Convention got national attention as their messengers voted for a boycott, joining the AFA. Last year the Assemblies of God did the same. Others boycotting include the Catholic League, Catholics United for the Faith, the Congregational Holiness Church, and Free Will Baptists.

In addition, the Church of God (Cleveland, Tennessee), International Church of the Foursquare Gospel, the Association of Independent Methodists, the Presbyterian Church in America, the General Association of Regular Baptist Churches, and the Church of the Nazarene have all formally expressed concern over the direction of the Disney company.

Also, pro-family groups, including Concerned Women for America (Beverly LaHaye), King for America (Alveda King), Christian Financial Concepts (Larry Burkett), and Focus on the Family (Dr. James Dobson) have all endorsed the boycott of Disney.

Why this togetherness? Number one, there is a mountain of evidence against Disney. They are truly out of the closet. (In fact, they've busted the door down.)

And secondly, the Disney company has chosen to spurn these denominations and organizations because Disney thinks it is too big to be impacted financially. Basically, that's what it comes down to. One Disney executive called our movement "a gnat on an elephant." Dumbo, no doubt.

Well, we shall see. Granted, this is the biggest challenge the traditional values movement has ever taken on. There's no doubt about it. However, I can't remember the last time so many Christians joined together in a concentrated effort to boycott one company.

Will it work? In time, I think so. How long before Michael Eisner and Disney come to their senses? For their sake, I hope soon. You see, it has been AFA's experience that boycotts can – and often do – snowball … not always, but many times this is the case. And once people's buying habits change because you have attacked their fundamental moral beliefs so often, it is very, very difficult to get back in their good graces, even if you do stop producing offensive material.

For 20 years, AFA has been a leader in the effort to restore the moral value system that made America great, and it is indeed refreshing to see such a unified stand in the Christian community. Let's work to see that the boycott is successful. And let's pray – as only those who trust and follow Jesus Christ can – that God might change the hearts of those in leadership at Disney. What a great, great testimony that would be, my brothers and sisters.

WHISKEY, A SMOKE, AND SOME CHANGE ... A SAD LEGACY FOR "THE CHAIRMAN"

July 1998 – With the possible exception of Elvis Presley, no other entertainer captured the hearts of Americans during this century more than did Frank Sinatra. I was vacationing with the family in May when CNN reported the news of Sinatra's death. Although being a child of the '70s, I could only name a couple of his tunes – "New York, New York" and "I Did It My Way" come to mind – it was still kind of sad seeing an American icon pass away. The Italian boy from Hoboken, New Jersey, made it big. He could sing, no doubt about that. Frankly (if you'll excuse the pun), I had no idea Frank Sinatra had accomplished so much in his 83 years. Albums, movies – this man lived what a lot of people call the ultimate "American dream." Fame. Fortune. Millions of records sold. Everybody loved Frank Sinatra.

A few days after his death, the funeral was a major news story. The television cameras captured a Who's Who from Hollywood, Washington, and New York, paying their last respects to their friend, the man they called "The Chairman of the Board." The day after his burial, I was reading about the service. It seems Mr. Sinatra's daughter decided to put three items in his coffin as he was laid to rest in the Southern California soil – things she thought the great entertainer would want to take with him if he could. The items were: a bottle of Jack Daniel's, a pack of Camel cigarettes, and 10 dimes. That was it. Some whiskey, a smoke, and some change to call home. I had to read the paragraph twice.

Later that night I was telling Alison about this. She looked at me with surprise and said, "What?"

"That's what they said," I responded.

"How sad. You would think they would have put something more important and more meaningful in his coffin."

"Well, yeah, I guess. But then, from what I've read, those things kind of symbolized his lifestyle. Drinking, partying, hanging out with the guys … that was his public persona. But you're right. Kind of depressing, isn't it?"

"If that's what your family remembers you for, that's real depressing."

That made me think about what I would like placed in my coffin if I should ever die. (According to medical experts I've talked to, there is a 70% chance this could happen at some point in my life. That statistic has a 30% margin of error, according to these same medical experts.)

How about my Bible? Yes, I'd say the Scriptures are very important to me, but it might be misleading to put them in the casket as if to say I treated the Bible as one of the three most important items in my life. It would look good. Real spiritual. Would it be honest? Truth is, I need to read and cherish the Bible more.

How about a picture of my family? I love my wife and three children dearly. And I am a pretty good father, if I do say so myself. I think Alison and the kids would agree. So to put a photograph of my family in with me would be true to what was important in my life.

Now, what else? Perhaps this personal computer I am now writing on, since I spend so much time in front of it. But if you include the screen, keyboard, speakers. and printer, you're talking about a much bigger coffin than I need or am willing to pay for with my life/death insurance monies that I would want Alison and the kids to have. Besides, it would probably be real hard to close.

What about an American flag? I love this country very much. In my mind, America, even with all her faults, is still the greatest country in the world.

You know, the truth of the matter is, we can't take anything with us when we pass from this world to the next – anything material, anyway. The Egyptian pharaohs tried to do this, take everything with them. That's why we have the great pyramids. But you know what? While I appreciate the hard work and building skill of the ancient Egyptians as much as anyone, really, all that work was for nothing. As archeologists have dug into these tombs, they have discovered the possessions still there. Perhaps you've been to one of the traveling exhibitions of these artifacts and seen them for yourself. Although very powerful men, even the pharaohs could not take their riches and treasures with them.

Later in my conversation with Alison, I made an observation. It was something I said without too much thought … just one of those driving-down-the-road-you-can-say-anything-to-your-wife-and-she'll-accept-it things. Said I, "You know, when you boil it all down, what really matters is: Do you believe in Jesus, and do you care for others? That seems to be the bottom line to me."

Alison agreed. (Smart woman, Alison.)

I know that there are a lot of variables and many additional concerns and passions in life for most of us. There's nothing wrong with that. However, in the final analysis, that about sums up our purpose in life.

Jesus was asked in Matthew 22:36, "*Teacher, which is the great commandment in the Law?*"

In verses 37-40, Jesus replied to the man: "'*You shall love the Lord your God with all your heart, and with all your soul, and with all your mind.' This is the great and foremost commandment. The second is like it, 'You shall love your neighbor as yourself.' On these two commandments depend the whole Law and the Prophets.*"

"You can't take it with you when you die" is a wise and truthful saying. Isn't that good? Well, you can thank me for it. I made it up one day while I was driving down the road just letting great thoughts roll off my tongue as Alison listened dutifully – and balanced our checkbook.

She then remarked, "Well, from the looks of this checkbook, that's not going to be a problem."

Smart woman, that Alison.

Frank Sinatra will long be remembered for his wonderful, God-given voice. But when he sang "I Did It My Way," I couldn't help but sense a ring of arrogance and pride. I don't want to live life my way. I've tried it. My way is failure. By God's grace I want to live *His* Way – the way of joy and contentment here on Earth, and ultimately, eternal life with my Savior. When I face my final curtain, I don't want to wake up in Sinatra's "New York, New York" but in God's New Jerusalem, the real "city that doesn't sleep."

2,000 YEARS ... 6,000 MILES ... AND I'M HOME

May 1999 – My dad served as pastor of several Methodist churches from the mid-'60s until 1977, when he founded what is today called American Family Association. During that time, he also began to lead tour groups to Israel – the Holy Land. His first "group" consisted of four people. Not very impressive to the Israeli Department of Tourism. But they did have plenty of space to stretch out on the bus. Since that time, he has led 23 groups of American Christian pilgrims to the little country, which sits at the crossroads of three continents – Europe, Africa, and Asia – and is holy ground to three major world religions – Islam, Judaism, and of course, Christianity.

I remember when Dad would get home from those 10- to 12-day trips, how he would tell of the sights, sounds, and people of the Holy Land – Mount Carmel, Nazareth, or a boat ride on the Sea of Galilee. He would talk of Jericho, the Mount of Olives, the Garden of Gethsemane, and how he had baptized someone in the Jordan River. And he would talk of Calvary and the empty Garden Tomb. Then when I was 12 years old, Dad took me along. The most vivid memory I have of that 1975 journey was actually walking on the stone path Jesus would have walked on the night He was arrested in Gethsemane and taken to the house of Caiaphas. You can still walk that path today in Jerusalem. You can visualize the angry mob.

Well, in 1998, Dad told my brother Mark and me that he had made his last trip to Israel, and if we wanted to continue the family tradition of leading tour groups, it would be up to us. So in March, Mark and I left New York City with 49 other Americans for whom we were personally responsible. It's a daunting feeling knowing that for those going with you, this trip is unlike any other they will ever take. This isn't Hawaii. This isn't a cruise. This isn't England. This is the place where Jesus lived. Where Christ walked. Where He taught. Where He fished. Where He helped his dad build tables, chairs, and – perhaps – wooden mangers. This is where followers of Jesus go to experience joy and solitude … sorrow and happiness. This isn't just *any* trip. This is a pilgrimage.

I love to travel. I love to see new places and experience different cultures – except for the food. I like American food. To be more specific, I like country cookin'. Aside from my family, that's the one thing I miss most while traveling in other countries. Instead of ham and eggs for breakfast, in Israel I have tuna fish and scrambled eggs. When I tell people that, they look at me like I'm sick. Well, I never thought I would do it either, but you adapt – to a point. I don't put ketchup on the tuna, for example, like some sick people do here in America. But the Holy Land is the only place I've been in the world – and I've traveled quite a bit – where I feel like I am somewhat at home while being a great sea, one ocean, and many thousands of miles from my beloved Mississippi. It's a spiritual sense of being home, I suppose. Knowing that, of all the places in the world Jesus could have been born and raised and conducted His ministry, this is the place He decided on. And some 2,000 years later, I have the privilege of seeing and experiencing these same places.

When I returned home from this latest pilgrimage, our church's Passion play began the very next night. I played Peter once again. This is a musical drama, so I am intentionally left out of any speaking/singing roles. (Wasted talent, I know, but no one else sees it.) The signature of our church is this annual pageant. We usually draw over 4,000 people to our auditorium during the seven performances. This time we had over 50 people decide to give their hearts to Jesus after seeing the life of Christ depicted in dramatic form and hearing the clear gospel presented. Many more renewed their vows to the Lord. During the pageant, I thought how ironic it was that I had been seeing the real Jerusalem just a few days earlier, and now I was on a stage playing as if I were in Jerusalem. How awesome, that the message of the love of God for mankind – which began in a small stable in Bethlehem – continues to be proclaimed today on a small stage in Tupelo, Mississippi, USA. And God still moves on the hearts of people through the power of His Holy Spirit. Wow!

Maybe you, too, have had the great joy of traveling to the Holy Land. If not, it is my desire that one day you will be able to.

TAKE YOUR BEST SHOT

May 2000 – I guess I should be scared of myself. That's what many in the media say anyway. So I go to the mirror every once in a while and just stare at myself. Sometimes I talk to the man in the mirror.

"You're one of the religious-righters, aren't you?" I ask myself. Having already answered the question, I have a rather mocking tone in my voice. I point into the mirror. "Sure, you are. Look at yourself."

So I look. And I try to feel. I try and feel the religious-rightness that is within me, that fundamentalism beast that makes me a threat to the rest of America. I wonder if any of my three children will become religious-righters. How did I get this way? What is wrong with me?

"Tim, go separate your sons, please!" Alison says from the bedroom. She, too, is a religious-righter, although more secure about it than I am. She doesn't care what other people think. Never has.

If I'm this way now, just think how I will be after we go through the summer and fall presidential campaign. My strong feeling is that we – that is, people who identify ourselves as Bible-believing Christians – are about to be demonized like never before. And what's ironic – the people that are going to demonize us don't even believe in demons!

Seriously, conservative Christians are what is wrong with America, if you listen to the mass media – including both the news and the entertainment industries. Nightly television programs rip the beliefs of Christians and hold those beliefs up to scorn.

So take a personal inventory. You may be a religious-righter if:

1. You believe in the God of the Bible.

2. You believe in Jesus Christ as the only way to salvation and, ultimately, to heaven.

3. You believe the Ten Commandments are still relevant and that there are universal moral absolutes.

4. You believe that abortion violates commandment number six – "You shall not murder."

5. You believe that sex is right only within the confines of marriage between one man and one woman.

6. You believe that homosexuality is immoral and unnatural.

7. You believe in the Great Commission given to us by Jesus Christ.

If you said yes to the above, you are a religious-righter in the eyes of most Americans. And *you're* the real threat to this country.

Recently I read a column by syndicated writer Suzanne Fields, herself a Jew and one of the few nationally syndicated writers who sees this Christian-bashing trend and calls it for what it is – bigotry. She calls it "open season on Christian fundamentalists." Allow me to quote some from her column:

> *I rarely sit at a bar or restaurant, or in a political meeting on a college campus, or engage in a give-and-take social life in New York and Washington without hearing casual references to the religious right "wackos," fundamentalist "kooks," or those "nutsos" who follow Jerry Falwell or Pat Robertson. You won't hear anything like that aimed at Jews, whether Orthodox, Conservative or Reform – or the followers of Rev. Al Sharpton, for that matter.*

Why us then? There are many reasons I believe open bigotry against conservative Christians has become acceptable. But I think, primarily, it is because we hold up a biblical standard of decency and morality – and unashamedly say so. Many people hate that. It's like the sound of fingernails on a chalkboard. We say abortion is killing. They say, "It's a woman's choice, and you wackos should just mind your own business." That plays well in our country today. Real well. They see our beliefs as pushing our religious views on them, and they react.

And what makes it even more difficult for our side to combat is that Americans have long held to the "live-and-let-live" philosophy. Americans have a high regard for privacy. (So do the religious-righters I know, I might add.) So when you take those

Americans who genuinely hate Christians, and you couple them with those Americans who – while they don't really have any particular contempt for us – have bought into the idea that we on the "religious right" have an agenda to turn America into a theocracy, you get a combination that represents a majority of people in this country. Thus, the bigotry against conservative Christians is acceptable.

I don't have all the answers on what to do about this. We must continue to stand for biblical morality; to do less is to deny our faith in Christ and the Bible. And we must be careful about what we say and how we say it so as not to give our enemies more ammunition to use against us with the broader public. We must stand for truth – but do so with the love of Jesus Christ.

MY ADVENTURES
IN WONDERLAND

February 2001 – We are destroying speculations and every lofty thing raised up against the knowledge of God, and we are taking every thought captive to the obedience of Christ. – 2 Corinthians 10:5

A few months ago, my wife Alison and I attended a local community-theater production of Lewis Carroll's *Alice's Adventures in Wonderland*. What is appealing to me about the story of Alice is that it is so crazy. Masterfully crazy. But then, that's kind of my brand of humor. The cast of zany and twisted characters tries to make Alice believe that nonsense is actually *good* sense: the Mad Hatter ... the Cheshire Cat ... the caterpillar ... and my personal favorites, Tweedledee and Tweedledum – the original Dumb and Dumber, although I can't tell which is which.

Today, we live in a culture that reminds me more and more of Wonderland. And I'm Alice. I look around and see nonsense called "reason." I see wrong called "right." I see evil called "good." Take, for instance, this story from the Fox News website, dated December 6, 2000:

Opening a new front in the religion-in-schools war, two Cornell legal scholars are advocating the removal of abstinence-based sex education from public schools on the grounds that it violates the First Amendment clause requiring separation of church and state. Constitutional law professor Gary Simson and Cornell Law graduate Erika Sussman say the government is promoting a religious agenda – specifically one backed by fundamentalist Christians – when it allows public schools to teach kids that foregoing sex before marriage is the only way to go.

Huh? Did I read that right? Yes, I did. All together now: "Huh?"

Just because a sensible (and moral) idea finds its origins in the Bible, does that make it a violation of the so-called church-and-state constitutional separation?

Question for you Dumb and Dumber … uhh … Gary and Erika: What, then, do we do with the teaching that murder is wrong? Isn't that found somewhere in the Bible? What about teaching kids that lying is wrong? Can't do that if we buy your logic.

Did you know that in response to the results of teenage promiscuity, many public schools are going to abstinence-based sex education programs today? In fact, this same Fox News story reported, "Of the 69% of U.S. public schools with a district-wide policy of teaching sexuality education, about 35% require the abstinence-before-marriage model."

By "results," I mean unwanted pregnancies (which often lead to abortion) and the spread of sexually transmitted diseases, including the deadly AIDS virus. In fact, according to Centers for Disease Control and Prevention, nearly 18% of American women and 8% of American men carry the sexually transmitted virus known as genital human papillomavirus, which causes half of all cases of cervical cancer. When I read this statistic, I was absolutely stunned. Twenty million Americans – mostly young people – are infected with this virus. One out of every five women. That is staggering.

I don't know exactly all that Lewis Carroll was trying to communicate in *Alice's Adventures in Wonderland*. Bet he had a lot of fun writing it, though.

On the other hand, I know *exactly* what God was communicating in the book of Galatians when He gave Paul these words: *Do not be deceived, God is not mocked; for whatever a man sows, this he will also reap. For the one who sows to his own flesh will from the flesh reap corruption, but the one who sows to the Spirit will from the Spirit reap eternal life* (Galatians 6:7-8).

There are a lot of voices in this wonderland known as America today. Some tell us sanctioning two men getting married is a good thing. Some tell us legalizing more drugs would be a good thing. Some tell us that teaching kids to remain abstinent before marriage is unrealistic and wrong.

The bottom line is that Christianity and its moral code are under siege from every side. Let us not fall prey to lies that almost sound like truth. Let us always look to the Scriptures for what is right and what is wrong … what is moral and what is immoral … what is good and what is evil.

MOVING ... TOWARD SPIRITUAL GROWTH?

May 2001 –"Moving" … the word itself makes a lot of us physically ill – as in, "I'm moving, would you please come over and help me?" In this case, it makes the one asking for help ill, because he knows he must do it – that is, move. And then the one who is being asked to help somehow – mysteriously – often develops symptoms of the common "I-would-rather-die-than-help-you-move" disease that affects many people when they are approached.

Boy, could I tell you some stories about moving … I'm talking stories that would make the hair stand up on the back of your neck. But I will spare you here because I wish to get spiritual in a couple of moments.

Although I've lived in Northeast Mississippi for 36 of my 38 years, I have moved many times. Alison and I began in the married apartments on the campus of Mississippi State University back in 1984 with a tiny fold-out den and three giant cockroaches. We shut our bedroom door at night to keep them in the "kitchen." (It was about as big as your average shower.) Since that time, we've had three children, collected a bunch of stuff, and just moved into a new home. And like the campus apartment, the house doesn't really belong to me. I call it "the bank's home."

But back to the act of moving. My question is, does God *cause* us to engage in moving, or does He merely *allow* it – an act of our own free will? Theologians have debated this for centuries, with lines drawn between good people. If the Lord *causes* us to move, it becomes one of my big "why" questions when I get to heaven. I know a lot of you are with me here on this one. I'm not talking a first-question-right-off-the-bat type question … but perhaps after we've been there 10,000 years or so, it's something a few of us might bring up. I think the Lord would entertain it. I'll ask it myself unless, of course, that happens to be the day I am … well … moving from one mansion to another.

If, however, the Lord just *allows* us to move, I must be more introspective. Then I must ask, "*Why, Lord, do I do this to myself?*" My feelings about moving can be summed up with the words of Paul found in Romans 7:19-20: "*For the good that I want, I do not do, but I practice the very evil that I do not want. But if I am doing the very thing I do not want, I am no longer the one doing it, but sin which dwells in me.*"

So there you have it, readers. Moving is actually a sin. I don't write it; I just quote it.

Seriously, what moving does is make you go through all the stuff you have collected under your roof since the last time you moved. We are amazed, are we not, at what we find? Alison and I threw away a lot of things we never used or even knew we had. We didn't want to clutter up our new closets with junk. We wanted a fresh start so we could collect new junk. (If you are waiting on the cliche´ that makes this column something of value beyond a laugh or two about moving, here it comes.) It's the same way in life. Every so often, we should "move," if you will – take inventory and throw away the junk. I'm talking primarily about spiritual matters now.

Maybe you are the type of person who keeps your spiritual oil clean daily. We should all live like that. I admire people who are consistent with Scripture study and prayer. That is the way it should be. I've never really been that way, I'll confess. I try. For years, I would start in January reading the *One Year Bible.* You know the one. I usually lasted until the end of January. One good thing about that experience is, I basically know Genesis by heart. I can break down Genesis with you if you want.

So now I've resigned myself to the fact that if I can read a few verses each day – sometimes every other day – and pray during the day before I get tired at night, that is a goal I can reach without having to beat myself up all the time. The point is, in order to keep the junk from piling up in our spiritual lives, we must constantly be before God, allowing Him to show us what needs to be thrown out – or better yet, what never needs to come into our spiritual house in the first place. Otherwise, we will dry up. And I've been bone-dry a few times in my Christian walk as well. No fuel in the tank. And guess what? It was all my fault. God never leaves us or forsakes us; it is always we who leave and forsake Him. In our walk with Christ, we are either going forward, or we are slipping backwards. I'm convinced of that.

By the way, if you want to say a prayer for my spiritual growth, please do. I need it. I do, however, have one other prayer request: if you would, please pray that Alison and I never, ever – not in a million years – even have a fleeting thought about moving again. Perish the thought of going through that sin again.

FINDING FORGIVENESS
ON THE GOLF COURSE

September 2001 – I almost killed a man once. I'm not proud of the fact, but it is a part of my history I can't escape. Only a few people have known about it until now.

Back in high school and during my college years, I used to do a little golfing with my buddies. One summer morning, we were on the tee for the first hole. I placed my ball on the tee and took a couple of practice swings with my driver. (I always used the biggest driver in the bag, thus enhancing my chances of actually hitting the ball when I swung.)

About 25 yards from where I was teeing off was the tee for hole number 4, where four men stood, clubs in hand, ready to hit the ball down that fairway. To put this in perspective, I was aiming my ball for a green that would have been at 12 o'clock. The tee for hole 4, where these gentlemen stood, would have been at 9:30. Then, in an act that defied the laws of physics, I hit my ball directly toward tee 4. That's right, facing forward, I hit the ball behind me!

In a millisecond, the ball reached the tee, ricocheting off the wooden head of a club one of the men was holding. (I can still see it today, my heart pounding.) I didn't know what to do. What do you say in a moment like this? "I'm sorry I almost killed you. Can I please have my ball back to try it again?" That just didn't seem appropriate. I just stood there while my buddy Jim Reese said, aghast, "Wildmon!"

The golfer who had the near-death experience was stunned. As I walked over to apologize, he said, "Son, if you don't have any more control than that, you probably don't need to be out here." I understood his logic. So I finished my round of golf that day and never went back.

Recently, I read another story of failure on the links, involving professional golfer Ian Woosnam. Unlike me, Woosnam was able to redeem his bad situation.

Relatively unknown outside the golfing world, Woosnam was playing in the prestigious British Open in July. He had been on what one news service called a "downhill slide" in his career. But here he was atop the leaderboard, tied on the last day of the tournament with four other golfers, including eventual winner David Duvall.

This may well have been Woosnam's last opportunity at winning another major golfing championship. The newspaper account the next day read as follows:

> *Ian Woosnam was pumped as he stood on the second tee Sunday. After nearly making a hole-in-one, he was leading in the final round of the British Open.*

Bending over to tee his ball up, he straightened up to his full 5-foot-4-height and turned to caddie Miles Byrne for a club. Instead, he got the shock of his golfing life.

"You're going to go ballistic," Byrne told him.

"Why?" asked Woosnam.

"We've got two drivers in the bag," the caddie replied.

Woosnam knew immediately what it meant. He had 13 other clubs in the bag. With two drivers, that made 15. Only 14 are allowed. The two-stroke penalty he had to call on himself would knock Woosnam out of the lead.

"At that moment, I felt like I had been kicked in the teeth," Woosnam said.

When the day was over, Woosnam did fall four strokes short of the winner and was left to wonder what might have been, had one of the worst gaffs in major championship history not occurred.

But the responses of the two gentlemen involved here is what captured my attention. First, I expected to read that the caddie, Byrne, had found someone or something to blame for his mistake. But instead, said Byrne, "You want me to stand here and make excuses? There is no excuse. The buck stops at me. My fault, two-shot penalty, end of story."

How refreshing to see someone take responsibility for his mistake. I kept reading the story to find out what Woosnam had to say when he fired Byrne. Surely he would say what a bozo Byrne was and how he likely cost Woosnam his last chance at a major championship. He would have been justified in the eyes of almost everyone because everyone who followed the tournament knew what a fatal blow Byrne's mistake dealt Woosnam.

To my surprise, Woosnam said, "It's the biggest mistake he will make in his life. He won't do it again. He's a good caddie. He will have a severe talking to when I get in, but I'm not going to sack him."

The story went on to say that the crowd sympathized with Woosnam and rose to their feet and gave him a standing ovation as he and Byrne approached the 18th and final green. Failure. Responsibility. Honesty. Understanding. Mercy. Forgiveness. I think I've read that story somewhere before.

BEARING THE TORCH OF CHRIST IN AMERICA

October 2001 – When I was 12 years old, my Mama Wildmon took me on a trip to see my aunt in New York City. That was 1975. New York, as you may recall from your history class, was a very big city by then. Very big. Actually, my Aunt Helen and Uncle Harold lived in Cranford, New Jersey, which was, as I recall, about 20 miles from New York.

We landed at John F. Kennedy airport and then took a helicopter over the city to Newark, where my aunt picked us up. Talk about your eyes popping out! I will never forget flying over Manhattan Island.

At that time, Memphis, Tennessee, seemed like a big city to me. I had never seen *anything* like this before. It was staggering, the sight of endless buildings that reached to the sky. And there it was, just outside our window, almost close enough to touch: the majestic Empire State Building. This was all kind of surreal to a young boy from Mississippi.

While we were there, Aunt Helen was nice enough to take us into New York for a city tour. My heart pounded with excitement as we got in the car that morning to go into the Big Apple – all the sights we would see, places I had seen on television.

Only once as a kid can I ever remember being more excited, and that was in 1973, walking into Busch Stadium in St. Louis to watch the Cardinals for the first time.

At one point on our New York City tour, we stopped on the southern tip of Manhattan Island and looked out over the Hudson River to Ellis Island, where stood the Statue of Liberty. I remember just staring out, not quite believing I was actually seeing this monument I had heard about all my life.

When I asked if we could take the ferry to Ellis Island, Aunt Helen and Mama Wildmon looked at their watches, reminding me that we couldn't see everything in our short tour. I don't know if I should admit this or not, but I was actually about to cry at the idea of coming to New York and not visiting the Statue of Liberty. In fact, more than that, I wanted to go to the top. I let them know I really, really, *really* wanted to touch the statue for myself. So they let me.

Upon arrival, my grandmother (then about 65 years old) and I began walking up the stairs to the crown. There was no elevator. As we made our way about half-way up, Mama Wildmon told me to go ahead; she was not up to the climb. She would wait for me to go up and come back down. I hurried up the remaining stairs and entered the crown out of breath.

There was no one else there. I remember thinking, *"Here I am, standing in one of the most famous places in all the world, looking out over the Hudson River and New York City, all alone."*

All of what I had learned about American history flooded my mind. (History and social studies were my two favorite classes in school.) I thought mostly of all the immigrants from around the world and why they had come – and were still coming – to America.

I thought about the difference between freedom and tyranny, as much as I understood it. I thought about the words on the tablet: "Give me your tired, your poor / Your huddled masses yearning to breathe free / The wretched refuse of your teeming shore / Send these, the homeless, tempest-tost to me / I lift my lamp beside the golden door!"

Quite frankly, at 12, I didn't fully understand what those words meant, but I understood the general concept – the concept that America was a land made up of generally good people who valued each individual human life like no other country in history ... a land people wanted to come *to*, not a land people wanted to escape *from*.

A famous quote attributed to French philosopher Alexis de Tocqueville is this:

I sought for the key to the greatness and genius of America in her harbors; ... in her fertile fields and boundless forests; in her rich mines and vast world commerce; in her public school system and institutions of learning. I sought for it in her democratic Congress and in her matchless Constitution. Not until I went into the churches of America and heard her pulpits flame with righteousness did I understand the secret of her genius

*and power. America is great because America is good,
and if America ever ceases to be good, America will cease
to be great.*

The Christian influence on America is being lost. In fact, if we continue this slide toward secularism and paganism, we will become like Europe – empty churches. "Christianity Dying in Britain," read a recent headline on the Fox News website.

The future of America depends largely on the response of the church to the call of Christ. Will we be fishers of men? Will we pray for America? Will we be salt and light in our culture?

I remember that day inside the crown of the Statue of Liberty, looking out in wonder. How grateful I was to be born in America. How proud I was. May the Lord help us reclaim that flame of righteousness and fear of God that made our country great from the beginning.

HITTING THE ISSUES HEAD-ON

October 2002 – Someone once said, "You win some, you lose some, and some are rained out." Well, that's the way we feel here at AFA, with respect to some of the issues we tackle on a daily basis.

The issues I am writing about, of course, are the cultural issues having to do with morality. At AFA, we are committed to standing for what I call "biblical righteousness." That almost sounds sanctimonious in today's overly permissive society, doesn't it? Many Christians are hesitant to use this kind of terminology – "biblical righteousness."

To say it another way, we are fighting *for* what is right and *against* what is wrong, as defined by the Bible. But we are fighting within the American system – that is to say, writing letters, sending emails, making phone calls, using moral persuasion, using economic pressure on companies, educating our supporters on where our elected officials stand, and – certainly – sending up prayers to heaven.

As president of AFA, I do a lot of radio and television interviews. When I am opposed by someone – say, someone from the ACLU or a homosexual activist – they usually say that I represent a group that tries to "ram their very narrow view of religion down people's throats." That works with the audience sometimes. After all, who wants to be forced to practice another person's religion? I don't. You don't. But if you think beyond the rhetoric just a little, you will see the fallacy of that statement. The fact that a person takes a stand on an issue, based on religious convictions, should not disqualify him from participating in the debate over the rightness or wrongness of an action. That, then, becomes religious discrimination – the very thing liberal, secular activists say they detest.

However, I think we should think carefully about *how* we argue our case in the public, so as not to give those who oppose us any more ammunition than they already have with the general American public. We can, and should, argue our positions using non-religious language when we can. We do this in an attempt to reach as many people as possible with the rationale of the Christian position.

For instance, I appeared on CNN recently to give our thoughts on the decision by the Big Brothers and Big Sisters of America (BBBS) to force their chapters to accept homosexuals as mentors for young boys and young girls. I could have gone on CNN and said, "Keep the sodomites away from America's kids! This is a perversion straight from the pit of hell! These immoral people need to be washed in the blood of the Lamb today!"

I could have done that. Granted, it would likely have been the last time I was invited on CNN … but theologically, everything in those three sentences is correct. Homosexuality is called "sodomy" in the Bible; the act itself is a perversion of God's plan for human sexuality; and homosexuals do need to have their sins forgiven by Jesus Christ, Who shed His blood for *all* sinners.

Instead, I used words like "unhealthy" and "unnatural" in the short time that I had. Those words are understood by the general public. While most Americans want to think of themselves as being non-discriminatory, they still understand it is not natural for a man to have sex with another man. The body is not designed for such activity. And, as it is in most cases, if a human behavior is unnatural, then it's also going to be unhealthy. Consider all the sexually transmitted diseases among homosexuals. AIDS gets the most attention, but there are others that are wreaking havoc on that group of people and on the population at large.

So if you can register in people's minds that something is unhealthy, unnatural, and even risky, then most would have to reason that this is "bad" behavior – not good for children to be exposed to, and therefore a group like Big Brothers and Big Sisters should not be promoting it. Do you follow my reasoning?

One other point, as we carry on a national debate on cultural issues, is that we – whenever we can – turn the arguments of the other side against them. Confound them, if you will.

For instance, in the BBBS situation, I made the point that this group does not even think about allowing grown men to mentor 12-year-old girls for obvious reasons. You don't put a vulnerable young girl with a grown man to be her mentor. Why then would this same group demand that homosexual men be encouraged to mentor 12-year-old boys? To do this is to invite trouble.

Having said all this, let me also say that we should never be ashamed to just come out and say that we hold certain positions on issues because the Bible says it's right, or the Bible says it's wrong. I've done that before, too. And when someone says, "See, you are forcing your religion on me," I simply say, "This is what I believe. This is where I stand, and if you disagree, that is your right, but it doesn't change what the Scripture says."

In an ever-increasingly secular culture, one that seems more hostile to the Christian worldview every day, Christians need to know what they believe and why they believe it so that we can communicate it to the world.

TAKING INVENTORY, HAVING IMPACT

February 2003 – About every day, at some point, I think about my life and ask myself what God thinks of it. Perhaps you do this as well. Sometimes it's an honest self-examination, and then sometimes it's a dishonest self-justification. Sometimes I end the day with a peace that I have pleased God, and other times I end the day by calling myself a spiritual bum. But I often wonder if what I have done, said, or believed on that particular day was good or bad in the eyes of the Lord.

And just to be clear, I am a believer in the God of the Holy Bible; I believe that Jesus Christ is Who He claimed to be in the New Testament; and I know my salvation is not dependent on my actions or attitudes on a given day, but rather on the atoning blood sacrifice of Christ. But I am talking about my day-to-day walk with the Lord. Am I honoring Him with it?

God has never spoken to me in an audible voice. I've never looked up in the sky and seen a thumbs-up or a thumbs-down on my day. Really, one must ask, how do we really know what the Lord expects of us? Where do we look for specific guidelines we can use as a measuring stick to see how we've done?

Now I have always been a big St. Louis Cardinals fan. (I've concluded that God is as well, but I can't prove it.) In fact, I travel to St. Louis at least once a summer with my boys to see the Cardinals play. During the 1980s they had a manager named Whitey Herzog. He was one of the most successful managers in professional baseball during that decade, having taken the Cardinals to three World Series. In his autobiography, he talks about the demands he placed on his players – demands that led to their success. He says he liked to keep things simple and had only two rules: the first rule was to be on time; the second rule was to give 100%. That's it. Be on time and give it all you have.

Now I don't want to oversimplify the Christian walk, yet I look over in the book of Micah and see that the Lord has given us three seemingly simple requirements if we are to please Him in our everyday life. Allow me to quote Micah 6:8, where God is speaking to His people, the Israelites: "*He has told you, O man, what is good; and what does the Lord require of you but to do justice, to love kindness, and to walk humbly with your God?*"

However simple these three requirements may seem, they obviously encompass a lot. And they are completely consistent with the words of Jesus in Matthew 22:37-40, where He is asked which is the greatest commandment, to which He replies: "'*You shall love the Lord your God with all your heart, and with all your soul, and with all your mind.' This is the great and foremost commandment. The second is like it, 'You shall love your neighbor as yourself.'*"

The way I figure it, as long as I am checking my life against these biblical requirements and asking God for forgiveness when I fail, I am on the right path.

In addition to asking myself if how I am living *my* life pleases God, as president of American Family Association and American Family Radio, I also have to ask myself this question on a ministry level: Are we honoring Christ in what we are doing and how we are going about it?

Speaking of simple, here is the mission statement of AFA, as found each month in the front of the *Journal*: "AFA is a Christian organization promoting the biblical ethic of decency in American society with primary emphasis on TV and other media."

I believe the message AFA conveys – the cause we fight for – is one that God cares about very much. Although it may seem so to some, our work is not in the abstract. When AFA battles against pornography and the proliferation of sex and violence in the media, we are going against a very powerful satanic force – a force that often destroys lives. People get addicted. Trust in marriages is broken. Adults and children are sexually violated because of what pornography does to a person's mind and behavior. These are real cause-and-effect consequences of this sin.

By the same token, when we encourage media that edifies and uplifts biblical values, I believe we are also pleasing the Lord and fulfilling His commandments.

The question we at AFA have to ask ourselves often is, "How can we most effectively do what God has called us to do?" This is where we covet your prayers most.

Obviously, you are with us, or you would not be reading my column. You give money; you support the actions we ask you to take. You trust us. But we really need your prayers – daily, if possible – that AFA's efforts have a real impact in "American society," as we say in our mission statement.

ROE PLUS 30 – REASON FOR HOPE

March 2003 – My dad was a Methodist minister. At least once a year he would preach on the value and dignity of each human life. Rich, poor, black, brown, white, educated, uneducated – it didn't matter. In God's eyes, we are all the same. Dad used to say that God cares for the common ditch digger as much as he does the president of the United States. God's love includes the unborn, for they, too, are created in the image of God.

I was 10 years old in 1973 when the Supreme Court made Roe v. Wade the law of the land. Since then, some 42 million unborn babies have had their lives ended by abortion. That's about the population of Spain. The numbers boggle the mind. We must repent, and we must continue to work to end the killing.

If you are like me, you sometimes get weary of fighting the culture war. But we can't stop defending biblical truth. Galatians 6:9 says, *"Let us not lose heart in doing good, for in due time we will reap if we do not grow weary."*

Pat Buchanan defines the culture war and the Christian's responsibility this way:

> *Ultimately, our culture war is about one question: Is God dead, or is God king? If God is dead, as the European*

philosopher Nietzsche wrote, everything is permissible, and eventually, one will logically reach the conclusion of Paris' student radicals of 1968: The only thing that is forbidden is to forbid.

But if God is king, men have a duty to try, as best they can, to conform their lives to His will and shape society in accordance with His law. Defection and indifferentism are not options open to us. We are commanded to fight. ... For the culture war is at its heart a religious war about whether God or man shall be exalted, whose moral beliefs shall be enshrined in law, and what children shall be taught to value and abhor. With those stakes, to walk away is to abandon your post in time of war.

Even with all that has taken place in America the past 30 years, there is hope that things might be changing. Recently 1,000 adults were asked, in light of medical advances that reveal the unborn child's body and facial features in detail, "Are you in favor of restoring legal protection for unborn children?" Sixty-eight percent said they favored "restoring legal protection for unborn children." This is very good news. It means people who are in the mushy middle are changing their minds based on advances in medical science.

The survey also found that 66% of those polled said they favored nominees to the Supreme Court "who would uphold laws that restore legal protection to unborn children."

Frankly, I am surprised by the results of this poll. But I believe the Lord may be extending hope to the faithful remnant of

His people – those who have been praying, working, and speaking out – that America might be turned back to Him.

Thankfully, some things are going our way in the pro-life community. However, the killing goes on. So here are some steps that we can take toward restoring the rights of the unborn:

1. **Support crisis pregnancy centers.** If volunteers can sacrifice their time to minister Christ to pregnant women at their time of greatest need, the least I can do is support these ministries with my prayers and my money.

2. **Vote and educate others about pro-life candidates** who are running for public office. Often, not even 25% of Christians of voting age actually vote. This is a shame and a disgrace. Are we always going to get everything we want from the politicians we elect to office? The answer is no, we are not. Often, we will be disappointed. However, if Christians do not participate in the political process, I can guarantee you that we are not going to see righteousness exalted.

3. **Pray for America** – for our president, for the Supreme Court justices, and that the abortion industry would continue to fall into ill repute with the American people. Pray for the millions of women and men who have been party to abortions. They are carrying heavy loads of guilt. What a joy it is when we can tell these people about the love and forgiveness of Jesus Christ.

4. **Persevere until we see the end of abortion in America.** Keep praying, keep working, keep speaking out. In the words of President Teddy Roosevelt:

    It is not the critic who counts; not the man who points out how the strong man stumbles, or where the doer of deeds could have done them better. The credit belongs to the man who is actually in the arena, whose face is marred by dust and sweat and blood; who strives valiantly; who errs, who comes short again and again, ... who knows the great enthusiasms, the great devotions; who spends himself in a worthy cause; who, at the best knows in the end the triumph of high achievement, and who at the worst, if he fails, at least fails while daring greatly, so that his place shall never be with those cold and timid souls who neither know victory nor defeat.

THE SKY HAS ALREADY FALLEN

April 2003 – A friend of mine was talking to a business associate who said the main thing he has against the American Family Association is that we are always against something. "It's the same with Janet Parshall, AFA, even Focus on the Family – the sky is always falling with these people."

The person who was saying this is, himself, a Christian, and he didn't know what a close friend I am to the person he was talking to. But he was being honest. It was his perception of our ministry here. A misguided one, I would say – but his image nonetheless.

A few reactions to this:

First, thank God somebody is against the open immorality in the land. And thank the Lord somebody is trying to do something about it.

Second, as far as America's moral sky is concerned, it has already fallen. Just look around. It's obvious. Abortion. Pornography. Homosexuality. Rebellion against righteousness, decency, and proper authority. Open sacrilege and anti-Christian activity in popular culture.

Third, AFA is about doing good as much as we are about fighting evil. Christians should be doing both. In fact, one could argue that fighting evil is actually doing something positive.

Fourth, I wonder if my Christian brother gets down on God for giving us those bummer Ten Commandments with all the "Thou shall nots."

I once heard a popular evangelist respond to these same charges that he was always preaching against sin, and he answered his critics by saying this: "I preach against alcohol because I love the alcoholic and his family. I preach against homosexuality because I don't want to see the homosexual die of AIDS. I preach against abortion because I love the unborn baby and the mother."

In other words, his opposition to sin was not just to condemn, but was actually an expression of love and an appeal for those hearing to take a better way … God's way.

But who wants to always focus on negative news? I know I don't. I think our reputation for being an organization that is "always against something" is partly earned because of our efforts to hold companies accountable for sponsoring trash TV or peddling pornography. And we are still fighting that battle because it needs to be fought. And we are still having some victories on those fronts, despite what you may hear. (See www.onemillion-moms.com.) But we have also initiated what most would call more *positive* efforts the past few years, which many folks do not know about.

- AFA now owns and operates a 200-station Christian radio network called American Family Radio (**www. afr.net**), which plays inspirational music, informs listeners about what is going on in our country, and encourages them to get involved in standing for biblical righteousness in various ways.

- We have original articles and features in our *AFA Journal* each month, many of which focus on people who are doing something positive in the culture.

We only have one America, folks, and we cannot survive as a nation if we continue to embrace godlessness and immorality. Oh, the nation may exist in name and location – but the soul of goodness that the Lord has blessed us with will be gone. Over time, we will become weaker and weaker until we eventually implode with problems too great for all our money and all our education to handle.

If we continue to mock God, He will bring us down.

AFA believes – as did Nehemiah – "*the joy of the Lord is your strength*" (Nehemiah 8:10). Ultimately, the Christian message is one of joy … one of overcoming this world. It is Christ Who has won the victory over sin and death. And it is Christ Who has promised, "*Blessed are those who have been persecuted for the sake of righteousness, for theirs is the kingdom of heaven*" (Matthew 5:10).

So we "keep on keepin' on," as my dad likes to say, doing what the Lord has called us to do.

LIFE ISSUES DEBATE REVEALS CONFUSED HYPOCRISY

July 2003 – A few years ago, I called the editor of The Clarion-Ledger in Jackson, Mississippi, after the paper had published a pro-choice/abortion editorial. I wanted to talk to him about what he had written and see if I could get answers to some questions I had. He agreed to discuss the editorial with me.

First, I asked him when human life begins, and he told me he didn't know when life begins. "No one knows," is what he told me. I thought that a silly answer from an obviously well-educated man. It's not a trick question. Most of us learned the answer in high school biology, if not sooner. Life begins at the union of the egg and the sperm and will continue until natural death unless it is killed or "terminated."

He – I believe – simply did not want to answer the question because to answer that question would have given me a starting point to discuss when human life should be protected by the law, and he – being an obviously well-educated man – knew where I was going with my question. Basically, he was defending his position by pleading the Fifth. But I asked him again, this time giving him some options to choose from.

"At birth? Eight months? Six months? Four months, two days, seven hours, and thirty-six seconds? How about when you can see the heart beating at eight weeks?" I didn't want to be a smart aleck, but I was making a point. He would not answer. I told him if he didn't know when life began, shouldn't he err on the side of protecting the fetus – or whatever is growing inside the woman – that causes her to see a doctor, on the possibility that it might indeed be a human life since it was – indisputably – inside a woman's womb? He averted the issue and talked about leaving that decision to "a woman's choice." I told him, respect-fully, that I was talking about life and death here – not the choice between vanilla and chocolate – and that we don't give people the "choice" of killing other people under any other circumstances in America, save self-defense.

What I concluded from our conversation was that he believes ending the unborn human life is morally acceptable if it was de-cided by the girl/woman carrying the unborn baby. Millions of Americans hold to this view.

That seems to be the same "logic" on display in the Laci Peterson case, in which her widower – her accused killer – Scott, is being charged with her murder and also with the killing of their eight-months-in-the-womb son, Conner.

So let me get this straight. If a woman goes to have an abor-tion, it's not a human being worthy of protection – but if the unborn baby or fetus is killed by someone else … well then, it is human. That is precisely what famed defense attorney and feminist activist Gloria Allred said on one of the Fox Channel news shows I watched a few weeks back. Where's the logic in that?

I remember reading a story about a woman in Arkansas who was four months pregnant. While driving, she was struck by the car of a drunk driver. She survived, but her baby was killed. The state of Arkansas took action against the drunk driver and charged him with the death of the unborn baby. A felony. The irony was that the woman could have been on her way to the abortion facility in Little Rock and had the baby vacuumed piece by piece from her womb, and it would have been perfectly legal. Again, where is the logic or legal consistency in that?

For years, those of us who are pro-life conservatives have said the major newspapers, as well as the major television newsrooms, have a decidedly pro-choice bias (for the mother but not for the unborn baby).

Now a very interesting internal memo (dated May 22, 2003) has become public; the memo from L.A. Times editor John Carroll to his staff writers, reads, in part:

> *The reason I'm sending this note to all section editors is that I want everyone to understand how serious I am about purging all political bias from our coverage. We may happen to live in a political atmosphere that is suffused with liberal values (and is unreflective of the nation as a whole), but we are not going to push a liberal agenda in the news pages of the Times.*

I'm no expert on abortion, but I know enough to believe that it presents a profound philosophical, religious and scientific question, and I respect people on both sides of the debate. A newspaper that is intelligent and fair-minded will do the same.

This is refreshing to see. I hope more major news outlets will follow Mr. Carroll's lead, and in turn, perhaps, some credibility with millions of Americans who hold conservative views can begin to be restored.

THE LIFE AND TIMES
OF ... AH ... ME

November-December 2003 – Like a lot of you reading this, I get rather melancholy around Christmas. Memories of yesteryear that can never be experienced again cause me both joy and sadness. Please indulge me this month; I would like to tell you about my life. I have shared bits and pieces, but I would like to let you know more of my story.

My mom, Linda, and my dad, Don, were both born and raised in the hills of Northeast Mississippi. Dad was born in 1938 and mom in 1940. Like most people who grew up in the rural South during the 1940s, their families had to work hard just to make ends meet. They didn't have much, but neither did anyone else they knew. Mom grew up on a farm, and Dad was raised in a small town.

They both went to high school in the '50s. Mom was taking summer school chemistry at Blue Mountain College in 1960 when Dad asked her out. He was living in nearby Ripley. As the story goes, she turned him down twice – for legitimate reasons – before saying yes to a movie. Dad was not going to ask again if the third time had not been a charm. On the way back to the dorm from that first date, Dad told Mom he was going to marry her. One year later, he did.

I was the firstborn. Came into the world on March 6, 1963, in Houston, Missouri. Dad was in the Army at Fort Leonard Wood just north of there. A few months later, they got out of the Army and moved to Atlanta, Georgia, so Dad could go to seminary at Emory University. He wanted to be a Methodist pastor. And on March 6, 1964, my sister Angela was born there in Georgia. Dad packed a three-year divinity program into two years, while stocking groceries at night and serving a small country church on the weekends. In 1965 the four of us moved back to Mississippi, and the bishop gave Dad four churches in Tishomingo County. I'm not kidding. Four churches. Methodists do this to see if you are going to quit. Dad didn't. My sister Donna was born there on February 1, 1966. Soon afterward we moved to Tupelo, and Dad took a church in its infancy. It was a challenge, and Dad liked challenges.

Then on March 6, 1971, my little brother, Mark, was born in Tupelo. You read that right – March 6. If you have been paying attention, you noticed that three of the four of us have the same birthday. At one time, that was two short of the world record, which was five siblings born on the same day of the year. (Twins or above don't count.)

My growing-up years were the '70s. The things I remember about that decade include seeing the Vietnam War on the evening news. I remember how my best friend's mom cried when Richard

Nixon came on television to resign from the presidency of our country. I recall riding my bike to the drug store for a candy bar, cola, and comic book many afternoons. The U.S. Bicentennial was celebrated in 1976. It was at summer camp of that year that I gave my life to Jesus Christ; I became a believer. And then one summer later, 1977, I remember Dad leaving the pastoral ministry to start the National Federation for Decency. Some years later that organization became American Family Association.

In the spring of 1979, Alison and I started dating, and in 1981, we both graduated from Tupelo High School. Then on July 28, 1984, we were married. We have been happily married ever since. We both went on to get degrees from Mississippi State University. She was a good college student; I barely made it. After graduation, Dad offered me a job here, and I accepted. I have been here 17 years now. I've witnessed our staff go from 15 to over 100.

Since 1986, I have had many responsibilities – from writing scripts for radio programs to doing interviews on CNN, from writing columns for USA Today to speaking at churches and conferences all over the country. In fact, I was thinking the other day that, with the exception of Alaska, North Dakota, Hawaii, and a few states in New England, I have now traveled to and spoken in all the other states.

The purpose of AFA is to educate Christians about the growing influence of secular humanism and moral relativism on our culture, and to show them ways to get involved to fight back against those things and all the social ills they bring with them. That's why we come to work here every day.

Today Alison and I have three children – our daughter Wriley, 16, and our sons Wesley, 14, and Walker, 10. I also turned 40 this year. Forty means you should be halfway to paying for your house. We're only four years away from beginning 12 years of college expenses – that's if none of ours choose the five-year plan as I did. You got all those numbers? Good. Now have a Merry December 25 and Happy January 1.

THANKS, COACH, FOR A THANKLESS JOB

February 2004 – I was in the ninth grade at Carver School in Tupelo, and I had made the basketball team. There were probably 50 boys who tried out, and only 15 made the team. And I was one of the five starters chosen by Coach John McAdams. So in one sense, it was one of the greatest times of my vaunted athletic career. But soon after the season started, I received my grades. What was worse, my dad had received my grades. He had warned me that if there were any D's or worse, I would have to give up basketball. And algebra had gotten the best of me – and brought out the worst – in what was to become my less-than-vaunted academic career. And Dad told me I would be the one to have to break the news to Coach. He wouldn't save me the embarrassment or pain. I had to do it.

I didn't sleep well that night, and the next day I had a knot in my stomach until the last period, when practice time arrived. I was very nervous, but I went ahead and told Coach that my dad was making me give up my place on the team because of my grades. Actually, I almost cried in those few minutes. Coach

McAdams had empathy … said he was sorry about it but understood my dad's decision. It was the longest practice I ever watched.

In a lot of kids' lives, the most important people are parents and coaches. And many times, coaches are *the* most important adult role models and agents of influence because parents, for one reason or another, are absent. Sad, but true.

The other day, I was counting up the ball games our three kids had played in 2003. (I hope you are sitting down for this.) Wriley, my daughter, played basketball for Guntown Middle School (GMS) and now Saltillo High School. Combined, that's 25 games. My son Wesley played basketball and football for GMS, which is 25 games total. He also played a summer of USSSA baseball, which was 60 games, as did my 10-year-old son Walker, who played about 30 games. Throw in 45 church-league basketball games for the three of them, and you are talking about 185 various athletic competitions.

Granted, some games I viewed with glazed eyes and phony enthusiasm. But that, my friends, is a lot of cold hot dogs. A lot of diet drinks. A lot of popcorn. A lot of bottled water. A lot of sunflower seeds. A lot of gas. A lot of throw-the-uniforms-in-the-washing-machine-before-we-all-pass-out nights. A lot of energy spent. A lot of money spent. And a whole lot of time invested. Which brings me to the real point of this column, and that is to praise all the coaches – and others who work with young people – who invest their lives in our kids and try to instill positive values in them.

I appreciate the work of college coaches, all of whom have had to work their way up the coaching ranks, but honestly – most of those ladies and gentlemen get paid quite handsomely for their time. But the big-time college coach doesn't have to drive the bus home after the game, if you know what I mean. He doesn't have to stay late and make sure all the practice clothes are washed and gear is put away. And by the time these youngsters make it to college, they have already been through the most pivotal time in their character development anyway.

I am talking about the junior high and high school years. Here is where coaches really make a difference. And they don't do it for the money – not that I'm against making money. But if you divided up the hours by the pay (those who get paid), you would probably find many coaches don't even pull a minimum wage. No, they do it because they love their particular sport, and – most importantly – they love the kids they work with. They genuinely care about them. And the shame of it is, that doesn't show up on the scoreboards. Scoreboards are what we parents and fans see; coaches see the face behind the helmet. They see the heart behind the jersey. The same goes for the Scoutmasters, Sunday School teachers, dance instructors, schoolteachers, and others.

So to all you "coaches" out there – I salute you. If you really care about the kids, God will honor your efforts, one way or another.

As for me on that terrible day, I went home and told Dad I had done what he asked. I was heartbroken. And so was he. He called Coach McAdams later that evening, explained the situation, and said that I had learned a valuable lesson, so he was giving me another opportunity. Coach graciously consented to allow me back on the squad.

And thus began my vaunted athletic career, which (unfortunately) I have run out of space to talk about.

Perhaps later.

AT LEAST I GOT ONE THING RIGHT THE FIRST TIME

June 2004 – "Now let me show you something," said my lovely and talented wife Alison, as I slowly reversed my all-fours to get out of the front flower bed. Spring had arrived, and Alison was just itching to get out in that yard and stick her hands in some dirt. Yeah! So at her direction, I had been chopping the monkey grass back so it would sprout better. Cut off the old, get ready for the new.

"You have to be like a painter. You have to step away from the canvas and see how you've done so far. See how you missed this over here?" She took the knife from me and went to do it herself.

I picked myself up off the ground, stood up, straightened my back, let it pop a couple of times, and looked at her.

"Right," said I, with a look of concern. Then came the work-ethic cliches.

"Even if it takes longer, I would rather finish one section right than to do two sections and have to come back over the first section again because I wasn't thorough," she told me. Even though she was using first person, there was no doubt that she was talking about me. But I was being a good little husband, and she didn't want to scold me too hard, considering the effort I was giving. So she gently corrected me, using herself instead of me in the classic "Do it right the first time" line.

"Can we not think of a clever metaphor to use at this point – that's if you feel the need to criticize – rather than the same old work-ethic 'yada yada' my mom used on me for 18 years?" I said to myself. I thought I had done a fairly good job pruning the monkey grass, actually. But I guess it wasn't quite good enough. So I just stood there and took it. She handed me the knife and moved on to other yard chores. I went back to my canvas of monkey grass.

Smart married men have learned the art of "taking it." You just give some semblance of paying attention to your wife while head-bobbing in the affirmative as you think positive thoughts – like summer nights in St. Louis watching the Cardinals play. Anything to avoid getting into a disagreement or argument over the quality of your work. It's just not worth it.

They say in marriage, opposites attract. But for the most part, that does not fit Alison and me. We both were born in 1963. We both graduated from Tupelo High School in 1981, and later from Mississippi State University. She was right on time in 1985; I was a little behind in 1986. (Well, I was just being thorough.) We both have brown hair and blue eyes. Both have parents – all native Mississippians – who have been married for nearly 45 years. We share the same children. We both enjoy sports, travel, and Fox News. Both love Italian and Mexican cuisine, steaks, and fried catfish. Neither of us cares for Chinese food. And we're both night owls.

But then there are just a few things in which we are opposites. She likes novels; I like autobiographies. She likes cotton candy; I can't stand it. And Alison absolutely loves working in the yard. It's not really the routine stuff (like mowing everything down) that gives her life meaning. It's giving the grounds great aesthetic appeal that gives her a charge.

Me? I'm not there. Never will be. "Just mow it," is how I feel. But of course, just mowing would not be thorough.

Perhaps this ill feeling for yard work goes back to my childhood. When I was 12, I used to mow a couple of yards each week to make ends meet. Didn't like it all. Only did it for the money. Push mower, large lawns, humid days, and those tiny gnats that bite hard and cause welts. I hated to see the sun rise on lawn-mowing days.

I did a two-hour mowing job for five bucks for a man down the street. Tell me that wasn't child abuse. Five bucks for two hours in the hot sun. I would name names, but he is still alive, and it would embarrass his family and mine.

Despite our differences about yard work, Alison and I will celebrate 20 years of marriage on July 28, 2004. That's one thing I definitely did right the first time. My years with her – which began as high school sweethearts – have been the most blessed of my life.

For that reason, Alison will enjoy – and I will quietly endure – another season of yard work. I hope there are many more in our future.

MY FIRST VOTE WAS LIKELY THE BEST I WILL EVER CAST

August 2004 – Who is the first president you remember, and what do you remember about him? Do you have good feelings or bad ones? I was talking to my **Today's Issues** co-host Marvin Sanders, and he said Harry Truman. That would have been the '50s and black-and-white TV.

For me, it was Richard Nixon and nightly coverage of the Vietnam war on television, as I was born in 1963. I remember coming into my friend's house and seeing his momma cry the day President Nixon resigned on national television. Then there were Gerald Ford and Jimmy Carter. And after that, in 1980, a man named Ronald Reagan, former governor of California, was elected by the American people, and from the moment he took office – with the freeing of the hostages in Iran – the world began to change for the better.

Mr. Reagan was the first president I ever had an opportunity to vote for.

It's funny how these video clips and photographs we have seen of the Reagan years take me back to some younger days and joyous times in my life. I graduated from high school in 1981, married in 1984, finished at Mississippi State in 1986, and my first child was born in 1987. Those were all Reagan years. So not only is my affinity for President Reagan linked by my conservative politics but also by plenty of wonderful memories from that period of life.

(Pardon the self-indulgence here, but then again, it is my column, and I would guess that many of you in your late 30s and early 40s feel the same way.)

There are several reasons why I loved President Reagan and have missed seeing and hearing him these last 10 years. One reason was the respect and dignity he brought to the presidency. This is a man who would not take his jacket off in the Oval Office because of the reverence he had for the place. Another reason I loved President Reagan was that he invited my dad to the White House in 1983.

In my mind, Mr. Reagan was best known for four things:

1. He was a staunch anti-communist and strong on national defense.

2. He was a great friend of business and Wall Street.

3. He had a great sense of humor and a positive outlook about America, both of which were contagious.

4. He very much believed in God, the sanctity of each human life, and traditional moral values. In fact, I believe

Mr. Reagan's positive attitude and friendly demeanor were a direct result of his faith in God and his personal adherence to a Christian code of conduct. Let me share some quotes and comments that reflect what I mean.

"Our Nation's motto – 'In God We Trust' – was not chosen lightly. It reflects a basic recognition that there is a divine authority in the universe to which this Nation owes homage."

  –3/19/81, Proclamation 4826 – National Day of Prayer

"We can't have it both ways. We can't expect God to protect us in a crisis and just leave Him over there on the shelf in our day-to-day living."

    – 9/9/82, remarks at Kansas State University at the Alfred M. Landon Lecture Series on Public Issues

"To those who cite the First Amendment as reason for excluding God from more and more of our institutions and everyday life, may I just say: The First Amendment of the Constitution was not written to protect the people of this country from religious values; it was written to protect religious values from government tyranny."

    – 3/15/82, address before a joint session of the Alabama State Legislature in Montgomery

"I have been one who believes that abortion is the taking of a human life. ... The fact that they could not resolve

*the issue of when life begins was a finding in and of itself.
... If we don't know [when life begins], then shouldn't
we morally opt on the side that it is life?"*
                          – 1/19/82, the president's news conference

*"I know now what I'm about to say will be very
controversial, but I also believe that God's greatest gift is
human life and that we have a sacred duty to protect the
innocent human life of an unborn child."*
                          – 9/9/82, Alfred M. Landon Lecture Series

*"I also believe this blessed land was set apart in a very
special way, a country created by men and women who
came here not in search of gold, but in search of God."*
– 2/4/82, remarks at the Annual National Prayer Breakfast

*"America needs God more than God needs America. If
we ever forget that we are 'One nation under God,' then
we will be a nation gone under."*
                          – 8/23/84, remarks at an ecumenical prayer
                          breakfast in Dallas, Texas at Reunion Arena

This may sound corny, but when Ronald Reagan was laid to
rest in California in June, a piece of my life went with him.

WHEN LIFE STARTS GETTING COMPLICATED, JUST REMEMBER HIGH SCHOOL GEOMETRY

October 2004 – The date was August 9. The time was 7:47 p.m. It was a mission fraught with peril. Both of our hearts were pounding as I reached over from the driver's seat of our minivan, tightly hugged my lovely and talented wife Alison, and told her what I needed to say and what she needed to hear. I told her that the challenge now facing us – an imminent challenge (which is much different than an immigrant challenge, although the words are similar) – was neither her fault nor mine. But it was something she was born to do. And I also told her if I didn't hear from her within 30 minutes that I was coming in after her.

I had a lump in my throat as she got out, shut the door, turned, and walked away. I could hardly watch. Like a scene from a movie, Barry Manilow music began to play in my head ... but anyway, back to my story.

There was my wife of 20 years walking fearlessly into Wal-Mart, and more specifically, into the school supplies area – a place angels fear to tread on the night before school starts.

The first couple of years we had kids in school, Alison would have everything bought and packed by mid-July. You know how that goes. I never thought she'd be a last-minute mom, but here she was at Wal-Mart the night before school starts.

Knowing I was suffering with her as I listened to the Cardinals game in the car, she called in an eyewitness report from the combat zone.

"You are not going to believe this," she said. "Buggies bumper-to-bumper, stuff strewn here and there, there's no more paper … It's bad. Really bad. I'm not doing this again … Tim?"

"I'm sorry, Baby, Scott Rolen just hit another home run, and the radio was fading in and out. What did you say?"

"I said next time, *you* are coming in here to do this, and *I'm* sitting in the van. This is awful."

Yes, readers, it was back-to-school time.

I always know it's getting close in late July when Alison mail-orders the L. L. Bean backpacks for Wriley (16), Wesley (15), and Walker (10) – sophomore, freshman, and fifth grader, respectively.

As we all know, going back to school, especially if you are going to a new school – such as moving from the middle school to the high school – brings both excitement and anxiety. My oldest son is in high school!

We went to "Meet the Tigers" the other night at Saltillo High School. Wesley plays on the junior varsity football squad. After we met the Tigers, everyone was invited to tour the new locker room facility. Wesley had told me it had become clear to him and his fellow ninth graders that they were not exactly held in high esteem at the school or on the team. In other words, like all freshmen, they would have to earn their Tiger stripes. Some things never change.

As we went through the locker room, I said, "Show me your peon locker."

"Dad, what is a peon exactly?"

"It's a high school freshman. You can look it up in your peon dictionary in your peon backpack."

The thing I most remember about starting school – especially back in my Pierce Street Elementary School days in Tupelo – was having to wear those brand-new stiff and scratchy blue jeans in the typically hot and humid August heat. Couldn't run a lick those first couple of weeks before the jeans were washed a few times and broken in. But I tried. Looked like the tin man out there playing football with the other boys.

Also, I remember the first day I walked into my eleventh-grade geometry class and thought, "I don't have a prayer. My mind doesn't work this way." I had just passed algebra in summer school – after failing it in spring school – with a teacher who screamed and shouted. I'm serious. This lady was wound way too tight, and there were a couple of guys in our class of summer misfits who knew just the right buttons to push. If you could take the screaming, it was a funny show. In geometry class, I could hardly stay awake, it bored me so. However, I managed to pass. I would later learn to appreciate teachers and professors who graded on a curve. It's called "academic mercy."

Going back to school, perhaps more than anything else, reminds us of just how fast the years go by. Yesterday, Alison and I were taking our Wriley home from the hospital. Today, she is driving herself and her brothers to school. God help us all to realize how quickly time passes and how precious life is – especially the few years we have to impact our children.

Well, good luck, students! All I can say is, I'm glad I'm not you. I don't care if I do have a mortgage payment. At least the bank gives me the answer to the question, "How much money do I owe?"

SQUEEZED BETWEEN THE LAW AND GRACE

February 2005 – It happened on a stretch of Interstate 40 while I was traveling from Nashville to Knoxville a few years back. I was behind an 18-wheeler going about 70 mph. I don't like being behind a semi for many reasons, not the least of which is the way they are prone to jackknife … and the fact that they can literally blow vans – like the one I was driving – off the road. When big trucks and vans get into a match for road space, big trucks win every time. So I decided to pass.

As I made my way into the passing lane, I sped up to about 75 mph. As I got up even with the cab, I noticed that there was a Tennessee State Trooper in front of the truck … as in a law enforcement officer … the kind who can write you expensive speeding tickets, or worse – put you in jail.

Now I have known several highway patrolmen in my life, and while they are generally nice guys, they are generally nice guys who do not like to be passed – especially when you have to exceed the speed limit in order to do it. I don't like passing a patrolman even when I am not going over the speed limit. I have this fear that they are going to pull me over and write me a ticket just for showing them up.

Faced with this situation, I looked in my rearview mirror, seeing if I could get back behind the truck again. By this time there was a man in a sports car right on my tail pushing me to push forward. He looked about 35 and needed a shave. That's how close he was. He then leaned forward in his fancy leather seat and began to make hand motions at me. No obscene gestures – just hands-in-the-air really-ticked-off gesturing. And he was mouthing. A likely cleaned-up version of what he was saying was, "If you are going to get in the passing lane with your pathetic little family van, then pass, you idiot!" This went on for about two minutes, and 120 seconds of driving 70 mph while trying to keep your family van between a semi and an extremely deep Tennessee mountainside ravine can make one very nervous. And I was starting to sweat. As you can see here, I was boxed in. So given the choice between making Road Rage Roger even madder and passing a Tennessee State Trooper at 80 mph, I decided to slow down, as I also began to do some mouthing of my own.

Safely back behind the 18-wheeler, I thought, "OK, pretty boy, I'll let you pass. Now let's see what you do with that fancy Italian sports car!"

My lovely and talented wife Alison had taken a break from her novel and joined me in a hard gawk at Road Rage Roger as he quickly pulled even with us. I sarcastically motioned for him to go on. Alison – defending her husband's honor – did the same. He glared at us as he kicked that fancy sports car into a different gear – a gear my family van had never seen or even thought about. And then I did it. You know I did. I couldn't wait to. I pulled back into the passing lane and got behind my new buddy to offer him a taste of his own medicine. And when he got even with the cab of the truck, you know what Road Rage Roger did? That's right. His fancy Italian sports car moved back into family van gear. As he looked back at me in his fancy rearview mirror, I could not contain myself. I laughed as I motioned for my new friend to forge ahead and pass the Tennessee State Trooper. He chose not to.

The moral of this story is that things are not always as they seem to be. What's the old saying about not judging a man until you have walked a mile in his shoes? Or driven a mile in his family van – especially when you don't have all the facts. The world calls it "cutting people some slack." The Bible calls it "grace."

Now, I understand that perhaps I should not have reveled in Roger's embarrassment; you don't have to tell me.

Lord, forgive me. And help me to show more grace when, perhaps, I want to judge someone but don't know exactly what they are going through.

After a moment, I backed off and let Roger back in between me and the truck. Happy trails, Roger, wherever you are.

LAND OF THE GOSPEL
NEVER GROWS OLD

May 2005 – I just flew in from Athens, Greece, and boy, are my arms tired.

Get it? Flying ... arms tired ... Been waiting to use that old joke for a few years now. Weak, I know.

Seriously, my lovely and talented wife Alison and I, along with our three children, recently visited Greece and the Holy Land. You might imagine that it was a wonderful experience, and you would be correct in imagining that. It was my first time back since 2000, and the first time ever for our children.

Highlights from the tour (which we made with 48 other American Christians) included seeing the Parthenon in Athens, taking a boat ride on the Sea of Galilee, visiting Bethlehem, walking down the Mount of Olives, praying in the Garden of Gethsemane, and sharing communion at the Garden Tomb – a place where some believe Jesus was buried.

However, probably the most significant day for the majority of the group was the 90 minutes that we spent at the Jordan

River. Why? Because so many of them were baptized in the same river where John the Baptist immersed Jesus.

It was also a special day for Alison and me because our 11-year-old son, Walker, gave his heart to the Lord and was baptized for the first time in the Jordan River that Monday morning. God doesn't have any grandchildren, the saying goes. We all must make a decision to follow or reject Christ on our own.

I've written about this before, but one of the most beautiful places on Earth has to be the area around the Sea of Galilee. As a child reading those Bible stories about this legendary body of water, I imagined it sort of like Lake Michigan or Lake Erie. Actually, it is much smaller – seven miles across and 14 miles long, compared to Lake Erie's 241 miles by 183 miles. On a clear day, you can see all the way across the Sea of Galilee. From your hotel room in Tiberias, you can watch the sun rise over the Golan Heights. It is absolutely breathtaking to think this is the very sunrise that Jesus saw each day that He lived around this lake.

On our way back, we stopped in Greece again. We went to Corinth and saw where Paul would have spent his time there, thus prompting his writing of two books of the New Testament. Pop quiz: What two books would that be? I'm not going to tell you. If you answered I and II Timothy, you are wrong. In fact, you are more than wrong. You have also embarrassed yourself and your family and need to get back to studying the Bible.

On the last day, we took a cruise to the Greek isles of Poros, Aegina, and Hydra. They are quaint, scenic, and more my kind of Greece than was Athens.

Saturday afternoon we got back to NYC, and Saturday night we took the kids down to Times Square, where we had a pizza dinner for $70, which included two pizzas and some soft drinks.

While on the plane home from NYC to Memphis, I asked the kids to name the three countries we visited on our tour. They said Greece and Israel but could not name the third; they looked at me, puzzled.

"On this trip you visited Greece, Israel, and New York City," I said. "While technically a city in America, it's actually more like a country unto itself."

SIN, HYPOCRISY, CONFUSION ... SEE, I TOLD YOU THE BIBLE WAS TRUE

April 2006 – My email address is public, so as you can imagine, I get plenty of them – mostly just advertisements for Mexican banks, Canadian drugs, or items of an extremely personal nature ... extremely personal.

Between 5 p.m. and 8 a.m., I will receive around 100 messages. The first 30 minutes of my workday are spent clicking through emails and deleting 90% of them without even looking past the subject line. And because of the nature of my work and the fact that I am somewhat opinionated, I get my share of detractors.

A couple of weeks ago, I received an email from a young college student, Clark, who was upset with me for several reasons. He began by saying that our country's Founding Fathers were not Christians but rather deists. When I pointed out to him that deists believe that God is not *active* in the affairs of men, and America's Founding Fathers – even Thomas Jefferson and Ben Franklin – believed in Divine Providence and prayer, he changed the subject.

His other problem was the fact that I am opposed to same-sex marriage. He said people like me foster hatred toward homosexuals and that the AFA was made up of a bunch of fools. He later made some other less-than-positive comments, but that was the essence of it.

I told Clark that I am a Christian, and I believe in the Holy Bible as the Word of God, and *that* is where I get my value system. I cited the Ten Commandments and the Sermon on the Mount. He told me my moral compass was broken.

I asked him what he believes in. He told me he is a humanist and believes in the innate goodness of man. I told Clark that was great, but I wanted to know what that meant, exactly. How does a humanist define "good," for instance? He didn't offer a convincing answer.

Humanists basically believe that man is god ... not in a New Age, spiritual sense, but rather the humanist does not believe God exists, and therefore he sees life though a purely secular prism. Any form of religion, to the humanist, is man-invented superstition. It is unprovable. Humanists find Christianity particularly bothersome.

Humanism teaches that there are no such things as moral absolutes. While the Christian and the Jew would say the Ten Commandments are given to mankind by Almighty God as rules by which to conduct ourselves, humanists do not believe there is such a rule book for life. While Christians believe that to violate a commandment is to sin against God (which requires repentance), there is no such concept of sin to the humanist.

While one might not agree with the Christian view of morality (and even Christians sometimes disagree on context and definitions), at least we have something to point to – the Bible – and a logical reason why it then affects our thinking and our behavior so strongly.

However (as I found out with Clark), while a humanist finds fault with Christianity, he has nothing to offer as a superior moral value system. They have no moral value system other than the one each man makes up for himself, which, in the end, comes down to being a matter of personal opinion. And personal opinions, like noses, are something we all have.

To the Christian, morality is objective truth given to us by God. To the humanist, morality is subjective opinion given to them by ... well ... themselves.

What I found with Clark, as I have with other humanists, atheists, and agnostics, is that they revel in pointing out hypocrisy among Christians. And while hypocrisy is a bad thing, it does not negate the truth of the Christian message. It merely means that Christians are exactly what the Bible teaches all human beings are – sinful creatures in need of help from God. We need to be saved from our sin that separates us from God (salvation), and we need the power of God to live the life He desires us to live.

Clark and I went several rounds back and forth with each other. Each time I asked him for some resource outside himself to prove the validity of his beliefs, he would change the subject, usually with another criticism of Christians.

I challenged Clark that if the Christian value system is such a bad one, name a better one. He has not done that to date. But if you think about it, when Clark tells me my moral compass is broken, isn't he passing judgment on me? And that is precisely why he wrote me in the first place, telling me (with regard to homosexual marriage) I had no right to judge other people.

Clark, you are confusing me, man.

EVEN IN 2006, WORDS STILL MATTER

May 2006 – Perhaps you saw the same survey I saw the other day, about Americans and public profanity. It said that "we the people" are cursing more frequently and using words that were once considered taboo in public. I was probably 12 years old when I first heard the "f" word used by a neighborhood kid. I even asked my parents what it meant because I had no idea. Talk about an awkward moment for a parent ... Today, however, you frequently hear words such as this out in the open.

A few weeks back, I was on an airplane, and the 25-year-old male a few seats over was yakking on his cell phone, letting everyone in on his business that none of us cared about. Every 60 seconds or so, he felt the need to use the "f" word. (I don't know if that made him feel more adult or what.) Later, in the airport waiting on a connecting flight, there was a lady (about 50) talking loudly on her cell phone. I heard her twice use the "f" word in what sounded like a casual conversation. Then while I walked at a local park earlier this week, some teenage boys were playing basketball. One of them called another one an "mf" just as casual as you please. They were not in a fight; they were just talking to one another. Raw profanity has become acceptable in popular culture today.

Rap music – the most popular music among young people today – is filled with gutter language. They play it loudly in their cars. Movies and TV programs use hard profanity on a regular basis. In a way, we have become desensitized to profanity. This has been the goal of Hollywood for many years. There was a time before the mid-60s when foul language was not used on TV, in movies, or in popular music.

But today, many people mock you if you complain about public profanity. They say it's just the way people talk today, and the language one uses doesn't matter. My question, then, is why use words like "f" and "mf" and "gd" in public if language doesn't matter? Why didn't the teenage boy on the basketball court just say, "Give me the ball, John," instead of "Give me the ball, 'mf'?" Why did certain words come out of the young man's mouth and not others? I contend that most people who use foul language do so intentionally because they understand the words themselves represent rebellion against societal norms – or what *used* to be societal norms. Otherwise, why use that kind of language? It's an attention grabber. Then, after using profanity for a long period of time, it *does* become second nature – just the way people talk.

For the Christian, foul language is forbidden by the Bible. That is why using profanity in public was considered unacceptable before we became a post-Christian culture. Christian values and morals are now considered passé or old-fashioned to many Americans – especially the younger generation, sad to say.

In the New Testament book of Ephesians, the apostle Paul gives these instructions to followers of Jesus:

Therefore be imitators of God, as beloved children; and walk in love, just as Christ also loved you and gave Himself up for us, an offering and a sacrifice to God as a fragrant aroma.

But immorality or any impurity or greed must not even be named among you, as is proper among saints; and there must be no filthiness and silly talk, or coarse jesting, which are not fitting, but rather giving of thanks.

– Ephesians 5:1-4

In Ephesians 4:29, Paul says: *"Let no unwholesome word proceed from your mouth, but only such a word as is good for edification according to the need of the moment, so that it will give grace to those who hear."*

What I take from this is that we shouldn't tear down people personally. So, in the spirit of that biblical command, I don't desire to attack anyone. If we have criticism of someone, we can do so without attacking that person himself – and do so with the purpose of achieving a positive resolution to the problem. We can talk about an offense without mounting a personal attack on the one who has offended us.

Even though we know the standard, we are still human, and we often fail to live up to those standards. But the occasional slip is not what I am talking about. I wish it were. What I am talking about is a serious profanity problem in the general population. Sadly, I doubt we can reverse this trend. As I stated earlier, in many respects our American society has rejected the Christian moral value system. So this really is the way people talk to each other if they don't care what God thinks about the words that come out of their mouths. To them – to us, in our current cultural context – it doesn't seem to matter. But according to God's Word, words still matter.

LIFE GROWS SHORTER; QUESTIONS GROW BIGGER

January 2007 – Funny how life changes as you go through the years. For most people in America, it goes like this:

- Childhood is filled with wonder. Everything is a new experience. There is very little sense of time except that it seems like forever until Christmas arrives.

- The teen years are filled with friends and fun. We look for and find excitement.

- Singer John Mellencamp (in his song "Jack & Diane") says of the post-teenage years: "Life goes on, long after the thrill of living is gone." I don't buy that idea, although there is an element of truth there.

- Then most of us get married in our 20s, have children until we are 30, and then buy a minivan. I know some wait until they are in their 30s to marry, and some even stay single, but generally speaking, what

I have described here is how it works in the good ol'
USA.

- When you reach my current age of 43, you see that
  your kids are about to leave the home and become
  young adults. Pretty soon they will be having families
  of their own. The thought brings both joy and melancholy. But this stage in life also makes you think
  about what lies ahead. You see, 43 is halfway to 86. (I
  graduated from Mississippi State University – that's
  how I know these things.) And 86 is nine years above
  the average life expectancy in America, which is 77
  years of age. In other words, even at 43 – which many
  of you reading this consider "young" – I am probably
  on the downhill side of my time here on Earth.

What I am saying is cliché, but I will say it anyway: Life
is short. No matter how you cut it, we are here today, and we
are gone tomorrow. The questions then become: What do we do
with the time we *do* have? And does it all really matter anyway?

For most of us, this is where religious faith speaks. For me,
this is where I want to know what God says about these matters, and since God does not schedule face-to-face, question-and-
answer sessions in an audible voice, the best place to turn is the
Holy Bible. Now, you might ask, "How do you know there is a
God? And how do you know He is the author of the Holy Bible?
And beyond that, how do we know that Jesus was the Son of God
as Christians believe?" (These are very good questions – questions

that I don't have the space to go into here. But may I refer you to a short book I have recommended before? It's titled *More Than a Carpenter* by Josh McDowell.)

But my short answer is that I believe in God because of the order in the universe. From nature to the stars to the human experience here on Earth, everything points to a Creator and is consistent with what the Bible says about life ... at least to my satisfaction. The idea that our existence is random and without meaning or purpose does not make any sense to me. If you have ever studied the complexities of the human eye, for example, the thought that it could have been put together outside of something supernatural is not logical. I could go on and on, but you get the picture.

Which brings me back to the questions I posed earlier: What do we do with the time we have? And does it really matter anyway?

Well, God says it *does* matter. He told us so in His Word, the Bible, which gives us instructions about how we are to live while we're here.

God desires that I obey Him. He says I am to love Him with everything I am. He says the main way I can demonstrate my love for Him here is to love other people. He says my first love on Earth should be my wife. My second love on Earth should be my children. So it seems to me that my time here on Earth is best used doing God's will, which is loving my wife, my kids, and my fellow man. I can demonstrate that love in many ways: I can serve; I can help; I can care; I can work *for* the things God stands for and work *against* the things God stands against. For the Christian, the way we use our time either pleases God or displeases God. And the Bible teaches that we will be rewarded in heaven for the good that we did in His name while on Earth.

Amen.

FREEDOM SPAWNS INITIATIVE, CREATIVITY

May 2007 – In March, I traveled for 10 days of sightseeing in Switzerland and Italy with 37 other Americans. There are many reasons why these countries, and Europe in general, are appealing to Americans. But before I get to those reasons, let me give you a news flash: The Japanese are taking over the traveling world. They are everywhere. On this particular trip, I saw as many or more Japanese than fellow Americans. If your state wants to thrive in the international tourist business, you had best figure out something that the Japanese would like to see or experience, because they will definitely get on the planes and buses.

But one reason why so many of you reading this are fascinated with Europe is that most Americans can trace their roots to that continent. Our ancestors who made their way across the Atlantic Ocean were Italian, German, English, Dutch, Greek, or Scottish, or they were from one of the Baltic or Scandinavian countries. And of course, Americans with Irish last names are everywhere.

No doubt, Europeans have contributed more than their share of greatness – especially with respect to literature, music, art, and culture – down through the millennia. Names like Michelangelo, Beethoven, and Shakespeare immediately come to mind. And let's not forget a gentleman whom many historians consider to have been the most important person of the last 1,000 years, and that would be Johannes Gutenberg, the German goldsmith who invented the moveable-type printing press, which made the written word available to the masses.

Thinking about these men while on our tour, I was also reminded of just how much the people of the United States of America have added to the progression of mankind in our relatively brief, 230-year history. From inventions to discoveries, the U. S. has led the way. Some of these include:

- Thomas A. Edison, born in 1847 in Milan, Ohio, developed the first practical light bulb.

- Alexander Graham Bell was born in Scotland and moved to the U. S. in 1871 before he invented and developed the telephone in 1876. (A couple of centuries later, "roll-over" minutes were created.)

- Samuel Morse was born in Charlestown, Massachusetts, in 1791, and [along with his friend, Alfred Vail] created the Morse Code. For the first half of the 20th century, the majority of high-speed international communication was conducted in Morse Code, using telegraph lines, undersea cables, and radio circuits.

- Henry Ford was born in Michigan in 1863. AFA's boycott aside, he founded the Ford Motor Company and was the father of modern assembly lines used in mass production. His introduction of the Model T automobile revolutionized transportation and American industry.

- Orville and Wilbur Wright, brothers, were born in Dayton, Ohio, in 1871 and 1867 respectively. The two are generally credited with building the first successful airplane and making the first controlled, powered, heavier-than-air human flight on December 17, 1903. In the two years following, they developed their flying machine into the world's first practical fixed-wing aircraft.

- Bill Gates, born in 1955 in Seattle, is one of the best-known entrepreneurs of the personal computer revolution. He was the chief software architect for Microsoft, the world's leading computer software company.

Those names are a few of the big ones.

These accomplishments are clear evidence that political liberty, the priority of education, and the free enterprise system – combined – will open the door to the best for the most. Free the individual from the control of other men and/or control from the state, and he will achieve great things beyond the imagination … especially if there is personal incentive for him to profit financially from his invention. Take away the opportunity for personal gain, and one can see how the desire to create, invent, or discover would be greatly diminished.

I also believe that God was the one Who blessed our Founders with the idea of freedom and then blessed them with the means to create and sustain the kind of country that would allow for all these wonderful inventions and discoveries to occur. If you think about it, the Founders were collectively great inventors themselves by virtue of creating a new kind of country that allowed for freedom of religion and freedom of speech.

Without the Lord there would be no America, and without America ... well ... we might all be blowing out our candles as we go to bed at night on some other continent.

Can't wait to see more of the world. But there is still no place like the U.S.A.

THE TIMOTHIAN CONFESSION

September 2007 – The older I get, the more the Holy Bible makes sense to me. Make no mistake, there is still much I don't understand and never will, but the basic message – I get. There is a consistent theme to the Scriptures, and that is God's relationship with man and man's relationship with God. Now you may not believe the message of the Bible, but if you study it some, you can at least understand what the basic point is, even though it was written by many people over thousands of years.

What I am about to do is give you Tim's understanding of the Bible's message. Here is how I would condense it.

There is and has always been God. The idea of eternity or infinity cannot be fully comprehended by the human mind. God is the one and only supreme Being Who created everything that exists in the heavens and on Earth. And by "heavens" I mean the universe and other galaxies. Although God is neither male or female, He is referred to in the Bible as the Heavenly Father. He is everywhere all the time. He knows all, sees all, and ultimately, is in control of all.

God is spirit. I don't know what a spirit is or what a spirit looks like except what the Bible says it is, and even *that* is not real definitive. But a spirit is a supernatural being that humans can't see.

God created man and woman in the form that we are today. We did not evolve from pond slime to apes and then from apes to man. The complexities of the human body alone are just too many to believe that we are the result of random chance. A fundamental law of science is that life cannot develop from non-life. With apologies to Gomer Pyle, Shazam does not come from non-Shazam.

God made man and woman with a free will. He placed them in the Garden of Eden and told them to enjoy life. He told them one thing He did not want them to do, and that was to eat fruit from the Tree of the Knowledge of Good and Evil. What is evil? Evil is, for the most part, self-evident; that is to say, we know it when we see it or experience it. But according to *The American Heritage Dictionary*, evil is defined as "something that is morally wrong; wicked."

When man and woman willfully disobeyed God, it was called "sin." This is what is known as "original sin," and the Christian teaching is that this contaminated the nature of man. This contamination was passed on down through the ages, and no human is exempt from it. This "contamination" – again, called sin – separates man and woman from God because He wants nothing to do with sin.

The spiritual agent for evil in the world is a being called Satan. Like God, Satan is a spirit. The Bible implies that before Satan was Satan, he was an angel who rebelled against his Maker, so God expelled him from heaven. He has a limited amount of power, while God's power is unlimited. The two war for the souls of humans.

God chose the Hebrews as the people He would write history through; thus they became known as God's "chosen people." That story is in the Old Testament, beginning with Abraham, who was the father of Isaac, who was the father of Jacob, and so on. These people today are known as Jews.

Then we move to the New Testament, which is where the expansion of God's relationship to man moves from exclusivity with the Jews to include all people. God's message for mankind was brought by His Son, Jesus Christ. (Don't ask me how God can have a Son; I don't know. But He did.)

So God sent Jesus to Earth to accomplish two things. One was to demonstrate and teach us how to live according to God's will; love for God and love for our fellow man was His emphasis. The second reason God sent Jesus to Earth was to pay the penalty for the original sin. God requires a price be paid for sin before He will forgive that sin and restore us into a right relationship with Him. That is what Jesus did on the cross; He took the sins of the world on Himself and taught that all who believe and trust in this sacrifice would be forgiven and made right with God.

And finally, there is the promise of life after death in a place called "heaven" for those who repent and believe. That is the Christian belief system in 800 words. If you don't already believe it yourself, I hope you will study it seriously. Jesus Christ will change your life. Forever.

JUDGE NOT BUT LEARN A LOT

September 2009 – I have a question for you: What is the one Bible verse that you hear most often quoted by non-Christians? I will wait patiently here as the theme music from **Jeopardy** plays in my head and you ponder my question.

Given that I only have 800 words to work with here, I'll go ahead and tell you. The one Bible verse that every non-Christian believes is Matthew 7:1, where Jesus says: *"Do not judge so that you will not be judged."* People – even people who claim they don't believe in the Bible – dearly love quoting this verse.

How many times have I heard that come out of the mouths of people who are otherwise clueless about the Bible? I can be watching the most godless reprobate on some television show talking about the vilest things he has done, and when challenged about his behavior, he will inevitably say, "Well you know what the Bible says – 'Judge not, lest ye be judged.'"

This is the heathen's trump card. It's supposed to end all discussion. It's one verse from a book they otherwise scoff at. He doesn't have any regard for what that same Bible says about the wrongness of his behavior in the first place – does not read or study the Bible – yet he knows somewhere in the Christian

Scripture it says something about not judging others, and that sure comes in handy.

Another verse commonly used among Christians themselves, when someone is caught doing something contrary to the teachings of the Bible, is this (again, the words of Jesus): "*He who is without sin among you, let* him *be the first to throw a stone at her*" (John 8:7).

This was a theme used at the recent funeral service in Nashville for slain football star Steve McNair, who was murdered by a young woman with whom he was having an adulterous affair.

Bishop Joseph W. Walker III told thousands of people, among them family members, fans, and more than 50 former teammates, gathered at Mount Zion Baptist Church: "Drop your stone the next time you write about Steve McNair. Drop your stone the next time you text somebody. Drop your stone the next time you Twitter. Drop your stone, those of you in the barbershops, the beauty shops, those of you walking the streets on the corner – drop your stone."

I once heard a pastor give some good advice about reading the Bible. He said when using a verse to make a point, always read the paragraph the verse is found in. In other words, put the verse in its right perspective. By understanding the context of a verse, we can better understand the real meaning or point of what is being said or communicated.

The point of Matthew 7:1, about not judging others, is that we should each guard against self-righteousness, understanding that we all are weak human beings and capable of the same wrongdoing we are condemning in others. We must constantly examine our own hearts, attitudes, and actions, and compare our lives to the standards that God expects us to follow, as laid out in the Sermon on the Mount and the Ten Commandments. And when we sin – that is, fail to live up to those standards – we must repent before God and strive, with His help, to do better tomorrow.

As for the admonition of Bishop Walker at the service for Steve McNair – talk about a man put in an awkward position.... Here he was trying to console the wife and children of a man who died while cheating on them. What do you say to the family who feels betrayed, and what do you say to those watching the funeral?

The verse about stone throwing is found in the beginning of John 8. Here the Hebrew scribes and Pharisees were trying to stump this new teacher – Jesus, a Jew – into contradicting the Law of Moses, which stated that the woman caught in adultery should be stoned. Jesus turned the test around on them and used that experience to teach her accusers a lesson about self-righteousness. But He also told the woman, after saying He did not condemn her, "*Go. From now on sin no more*" (John 8:11).

He called her adultery "sin." Notice He did not say, "Go, and make no more mistakes." When we call sin "mistakes," we diminish the seriousness of what has occurred, for which the sinner is responsible. Jesus came to Earth to die on a cross to pay the price for our sins – not our mistakes. Notice Jesus did not say to her, "Go. It's only sex." No, He called adultery "sin" and ordered her not to do it anymore. Jesus judged the wrongness of the action, but He did not condemn the person. He offered her an opportunity to repent and start anew. He is our example.

Steve McNair's ending was a tragedy in many ways. Let's at least learn a lesson from it. Stay away from sin.

IT TOOK HIM ONLY A WEEK ...

January 2010 – I remember sitting in the pew listening to my dad preach when I was a kid. Most of us don't remember many sermons from when we were young, even if our daddy was the minister. You just hope all the messages you can't remember sank down into your soul somewhere and make you a better Christian today.

Mostly, I remember catch phrases or talking points, if you will. Every so often, Dad would have a message on the meaning and purpose of life. In that context, he would talk about the Bible and the origin of life. The catch phrase I remember was something like this: "It takes more faith to believe in atheistic evolution than it does to believe that God created everything."

Do you believe that there is an intelligent mind behind the world and our universe? Or do you believe that the world and human existence is a matter of chance or happenstance? And do you believe "happenstance" is even a word, or do you believe – as I do – that it is a word that slowly evolved over the last few years? (We will deal with that last question another day.)

There have been volumes written on "creation versus evolution." I believe the first sentence of the Bible, Genesis 1:1: "*In the beginning God created the heavens and the earth.*" But to debate creation and evolution is not my purpose here. My purpose is to share with you some information from a fascinating new book titled *Who Built the Moon?* written by British researchers Christopher Knight and Alan Butler. These gentlemen say that their study had no religious component, and both describe themselves as "dyed-in-the-wool agnostics." What these guys did was study everything about the moon … everything.

"Our first realization," said Butler, "is that all experts agree that the moon is a highly improbable object, and it has been nothing less than an incubator for life on earth. Quite simply, we humans would not be here if the moon had not been exactly the size it is in the various positions it has held over the last 4.5 billion years."

(Note to reader: I don't know how the gents got the number "4.5 billion years," but it is not germane to what they discovered.)

Knight and Butler then noticed some very odd mathematical relationships between the size of the moon, the earth, and the sun. The orbital characteristics of the moon and the earth, they say, are unlikely to exist by chance alone. For example, the earth revolves 366 times in one orbit of the sun, and the earth is 366% larger than the moon. Conversely, the moon takes 27.32 days to orbit the earth and is 27.32% of earth's size.

"There is no possible relationship between the relative size of the earth and the moon and their orbital characteristics, yet the numbers are the same. And that was just the first of many such underlying patterns," said Knight. "The number 366 was the basis of the ancient measuring system we have reconstructed, and that number keeps popping up, along with a small group of round numbers such as 400 and 10,000. For example, the moon is 400 times closer to the earth than the sun and exactly 400 times smaller than the sun. And in 366 orbits of the moon, the earth experiences 10,000 days."

"We were confused at first," admitted Butler. "Where there should have been random, disconnected numbers there were beautifully harmonious relationships and repeating patterns. It struck us as though we were looking at some kind of engineering blueprint involving the earth and the moon's interaction around the sun."

As if this weren't enough, says the press release about the book, Knight and Butler made an even more surprising discovery. The metric system, the scientific measurement that is now universally adopted across the world, appears to have been created specifically to highlight the peculiarities of the moon. For example, the earth is 109.3 times smaller than the sun, while the circumference of the moon (when measured in kilometers) is 10,930 km! Also, the moon is turning at exactly 1% of the earth's spin, which gives a speed at the lunar equator of precisely 400 kilometers per hour.

Again, quoting from the press release: "According to the pair, there can be only one logical explanation. Some agency saw the life-bearing potential of the earth/sun system and added the moon as a means to create and nurture life. But the same agency did much more. It made certain that the resulting mathematics would be particularly relevant to a species with 10 fingers and also in the absolute knowledge of the eventual use of the metric system."

To be certain, these are compelling revelations.

My interpretation: "*In the beginning God created the heavens and the earth.*"

MY DAD ... CUT FROM A DIFFERENT CLOTH

May 2010 – In the fall of 1976, I was a seventh grader at Southaven Junior High School in Southaven, Mississippi. I was new to the school and didn't know anyone.

Although I was too skinny, I went out for the football team anyway. One day before practice, I was sitting in front of my locker minding my own business, when one of the other boys decided to take the shoestrings out of his cleats and swat me with them. I didn't know the guy and had never spoken a word to him. I had absolutely no relationship with him. But that didn't suppress his urge to whip me with his long, nylon shoestrings.

He came over to my locker where I was sitting and swatted me once. I was stunned. It felt like a bee sting on my arm. He laughed.

"What are you ..." I stammered.

He swatted me again.

By then, it was clear that his only motivation was to goad me into a fight.

I looked around for help. No coach in sight.

"Whatcha gonna do about it?" he taunted.

Sensing a fight brewing, the other boys began to huddle around and egg on the conflict.

I thought about my situation for a second and stood up. I didn't want to fight this dude. I didn't even know how to fight. But I decided I had to stand up for myself. Obviously no one else would. The other boys didn't even know my name, much less care about the injustice of the situation. And so they began to taunt me and encourage the other kid.

His name was Nelson, I learned. His friends called him "Nellie," as in, "Hit 'im, Nellie!"

But no one was yelling, "Hit 'im, Timmy!"

Talk about feeling all alone. My heart started to pound. Nellie threw down the shoestrings and put up his fists, insisting that we get on with business. I didn't want to do business with Nellie. But knowing I had no other choice, I took the boxer's stance as best I could and prepared to be pummeled. We exchanged a few punches before he landed a solid blow to one of my eyes, at which point I bent over in great pain.

Finally, one of the coaches pushed through the huddle of onlookers. Nellie stood gloating. I was doubled over in pain.

Coach escorted us both to the principal's office. You know the drill: If you get caught fighting at school, it doesn't matter who started it, both of you go to the office and normally both get suspended. It was an early, painful lesson in injustice.

The school called my mom, and she came and picked me up. She had already called Dad at his office at First United Methodist Church. He was the new pastor.

Dad came home to talk to me. As I began to tell my tale of great injustice, it began to dawn on me that I was much more upset than Dad was.

He stopped me in the middle of my story and looked me in the (black) eye. In his starched white shirt and preacher's tie, he began to preach a most surprising sermon to his firstborn.

"OK, I will talk with the principal," he said, "but here is what I want you to do the next time." I thought I knew what was coming from the young pastor. It would surely be the standard "Turn-the-other-eyeball" sermon.

But to my surprise, he offered this counsel: "The next time someone wants to start a fight with you, take your fist just like this." He rolled up his sleeves to demonstrate. "Take your right fist, double it up tightly, keep your head up so you can see what the other guy is doing, and then find an opening. Swing your arm as hard as you can and punch him right in the face. Defend yourself, Tim!" he exhorted. "There will always be bullies at school, and you can't let them intimidate you. Now show me what I just showed you. Go ahead; double up your fist and come at me like I was this kid at school."

For the first time in my life, I understood that my dad, Rev. Don Wildmon – graduate of Emory University and a man of the cloth – was, in fact, cut from a *different* cloth. I discovered that day that he was a man who, if he thought it was a righteous fight, would fight for what he believed. In fact, I would see him take his own advice many times in the years and decades to come.

Dad resigned as chairman of American Family Association and American Family Radio in February, after 33 years of fighting for righteousness in our nation.

And as it turned out, Nellie was a junior boxing champion. Who knew? Glad I didn't. Looking back, I think I did OK to hold him to just one black eye.

THE WORLD'S MOST
GENEROUS PEOPLE

July-August 2011 – *"It is more blessed to give than to receive."* –
Jesus Christ (Acts 20:35)

So my lovely and talented wife Alison and I are walking into
Walmart Wednesday afternoon when she gets a call from Wesley,
our 21-year-old son. He is on his way to a meeting at a local
church about a mission trip to Honduras in June. Particularly in
the summer, thousands of American churches will sponsor exactly this kind of trip to places all over the world.

"OK, I will give Dad the check, and he will wait for you in
front of Walmart," she said to him. So she wrote out the check
and handed it to me.

"How much is it?" I asked casually.

She handed me the check. I almost fainted.

"It's a 10-day trip, including airfare," she said. "That is about
what you would expect."

I agreed. But still, it was a whole lot of money out of our
bank account – money that could have been spent many other
ways. And for what purpose really? How does this expenditure

of time and money benefit Wesley? What does it benefit his parents who are paying for most of this trip? Wesley is going to a poor country in Central America for 10 days to help people he has never even met and whom he may never see again. What is the purpose of that? Where exactly does that fall on Maslow's Hierarchy of Needs?

In terms of pure self-interest, with the possible exception of experiencing another part of the world for cultural reasons, there is absolutely nothing to gain here. And yet, this is what Americans do. More specifically, this is what American Christians do, more than any other group of people in the history of the world.

The motivation to give money and volunteer time to help victims of natural disasters or to assist people in underdeveloped countries has its foundation in the New Testament. In other words, to participate in these things is an act of obedience to God. That teaching has been a mainstay of Christianity since its inception. Because the Christian faith has been the dominant religion in America for more than two centuries, it stands to reason that Americans would also be the most generous people in the world with their money and time.

No other major world religion practices acts of charity and compassion like Christianity. It's not even close. Hospitals, orphanages, schools, food, shelter … the list goes on. Catholics and Protestants alike carry on this work around the world. And they do so with absolutely no expectation of ever receiving anything in return from the people they help and serve.

In 2008, the *Journal of the American Enterprise Institute* posted on their Web site an article titled "A Nation of Givers." In it they delve into the reasons why Americans donate more to charitable causes and volunteer so much more time than do other people around the world.

Here are some of their findings:

- "No developed country approaches American giving."

- A study conducted in the year 2000 showed that religious Americans were 25% "more likely to give charitably than 'secularists'" and were 23% "more likely to volunteer" their time.

- Religious people do not just donate to their own church – they also donate more to charities with secular causes than do secularists.

- "Self-described 'conservatives' … are more likely to give [to charities] and give 30% more dollars – than self-described 'liberals.'"

- "In 2002, conservative Americans were more likely to donate blood each year, and did so more often, than liberals. People who said they were 'conservative' or 'extremely conservative' made up less than one-fifth of the population, but donated more than a quarter of the blood."

- "Charitable giving has generally risen faster than the growth of the American economy for more than half a century."

- "Tax deductibility [for charitable donations] is irrelevant for most people."

- "IRS records show that only about a third of people who file tax returns itemize their deductions – which means that most Americans ... don't even claim the deductions to which they are entitled."

The truth is, unlike Christianity, most religions in this world do not foster concern or care for other people. Most major religions have a fatalistic worldview and do not believe in a personal God Who cares how humans treat one another.

Christians believe that God is watching how we behave while we are here on Earth, and Jesus admonished us to practice acts of kindness, benevolence, and charity because doing so pleases God. The Bible does teach that those who live by these values will be rewarded spiritually and otherwise here and in the hereafter.

And the bonus is that it blesses us even in the present.

REASONABLE PEOPLE CAN DISAGREE WITHOUT HATING

December 2011 – I remember when I was a kid, my mama would correct any of us children if we got really upset and blurted out that we "hated" someone. She would say it was OK to "strongly dislike," but she would not let us get away with using the word "hate." I don't even think I could use the word to describe my feelings for asparagus.

The word "hate" is one of the most powerful words in the English language. Although we could not use it at all in our home, there is a place for the word "hate." It's appropriate when we show pictures of Adolf Hitler; Hitler hated Jews. It's appropriate when we show pictures of men wearing the white hoods of the Ku Klux Klan; the KKK hates black people. When we talk about such people, it is appropriate to use the word "hate."

In October a group visited Tupelo, Mississippi, the hometown of AFA, to protest AFA with an event they called "Give Hate a Holiday."

According to this group, AFA hates gays, lesbians, bisexuals, and transgendered people.

As president of AFA, I totally and completely reject this slanderous charge.

AFA *does* believe that homosexual behavior is sinful. The Bible clearly says so. This has been the teaching in all branches of the Christian church for 2,000 years. Only recently have some liberal Protestant denominations begun to reject that teaching.

In the book of Romans, Chapter 1, Paul is writing about the wrath of God *"against all ungodliness and unrighteousness of men who suppress the truth in unrighteousness (v. 18)."* In verses 24-27, the Scripture reads:

> *Therefore God gave them over in the lusts of their hearts to impurity, so that their bodies would be dishonored among them. For they exchanged the truth of God for a lie, and worshiped and served the creature rather than the Creator, who is blessed forever. Amen.*

> *For this reason God gave them over to degrading passions; for their women exchanged the natural function for that which is unnatural, and in the same way also the men abandoned the natural function of the woman and burned in their desire toward one another, men with men committing indecent acts and receiving in their own persons the due penalty of their error.*

This is where Christians get the idea that homosexuality is sinful. The New Testament goes on to label every single one of us as sinners. Homosexual behavior may not be yours, but the sins that condemn you are in there, and the sins that condemn me are in there.

What has happened over the last 30 years in America is that homosexual groups have tried to force changes on society that have been met with resistance. They have tried to convince people that civil rights should be granted based on someone's sexual behavior (a choice) in the same way civil rights should be granted based on someone's skin color (not a choice). And if you are one who does not publicly affirm the lifestyle of homosexuals, then you are – by their definition – someone who "hates." This is unfair, but this is how they frame the issue.

I believe most Americans agree with AFA. We do not believe in changing the legal definition of marriage to support two men getting "married." Thirty-one states have voted on this, and 31 states – including such liberal states as California, Oregon, and Maine – have said marriage should remain legally defined as one man and one woman. As a candidate for president, Barack Obama was publicly opposed to homosexual marriage.

As far as the military is concerned, there is a good reason why there has always been a policy disallowing homosexuals. Where do you put them? The reason men and women don't share showers or sleeping quarters is to avoid sexual temptation and tension that could break down discipline, order, and morale. Men and women are rightly separated. Again, what do you with men who are open about their sexual attraction to other men? It is not right to force straight men to shower and bunk with gay men, any more than it is right to force women to shower and bunk with heterosexual men.

Disagreement with the GLBT (gay, lesbian, bisexual, trans-gender) movement on theological or public policy issues does not constitute hate. Reasonable people understand that.

DEMOCRACY NEEDS CHRISTIANITY

March 2012 – In 1840, a Frenchman named Alexis de Tocqueville published the second volume of his two-part work known as *Democracy in America*, based on his travels through the United States in 1831. De Tocqueville was a political thinker, historian, and journalist. He was curious about this New World to which many Europeans were immigrating, and so he set out to observe and experience American life.

I encourage anyone to read this work. It's a very compelling account of life in America in that snapshot of time. There is much to learn about history from reading this outsider's view because of his comparisons of America to Europe. The popularity of *Democracy in America* was, in large part, because it was so comprehensive, and it was considered objective and fair by most historians and readers. There was no political or philosophical ax to grind. De Tocqueville wrote about the great, the good, the bad, and the ugly. Although I have not finished both volumes in their entirety, I was struck by this particularly poignant passage, which opens Chapter 15 in Volume 2, Section 2:

In the United States, on the seventh day of every week, the trading and working life of the nation seems suspended; all noises cease; a deep tranquility, say rather the solemn calm of meditation, succeeds the turmoil of the week, and the soul resumes possession and contemplation of itself. Upon this day the marts of traffic are deserted; every member of the community, accompanied by his children, goes to church, where he listens to strange language which would seem unsuited to his ear. He is told of the countless evils caused by pride and covetousness; he is reminded of the necessity of checking his desires, of the finer pleasures which belong to virtue alone, and of the true happiness which attends it. On his return home, he does not turn to the ledgers of his calling, but he opens the book of Holy Scripture; there he meets with sublime or affecting descriptions of the greatness and goodness of the Creator, of the infinite magnificence of the handiwork of God, of the lofty destinies of man, of his duties, and of his immortal privileges. …

I have endeavored to point out in another part of this work the causes to which the maintenance of the political institutions of the Americans is attributable; and religion appeared to be one of the most prominent amongst them. I am now treating of the Americans in an individual capacity, and I again observe that religion is not less useful to each citizen than to the whole State. The Americans show, by their practice, that they feel the high necessity of imparting morality to democratic communities by means of religion. What they think of themselves in this respect

*is a truth of which every democratic nation ought to be
thoroughly persuaded.*

To de Tocqueville, the emphasis on the Christian religion
in America permeated the whole society, advanced individual
and corporate morality, and was the glue that held the country
together.

Nearly 40 years before de Tocqueville, no less a man than
President George Washington had said essentially the same thing
in his farewell address:

*Of all the dispositions and habits, which lead to political
prosperity, religion and morality are indispensable supports.
In vain would that man claim the tribute of patriotism
who should labor to subvert these great pillars of human
happiness, these firmest props of the duties of men and
citizens.*

If America does not soon have a Christian revival on a large
scale, we will slowly die, and history will record us only as "the
great nation that was."

AN EYE FOR EVIDENCE

April 2012 – I have a friend, Frank Turek, who wrote a book titled *I Don't Have Enough Faith to Be an Atheist.**

I don't either, Frank.

My dad tells the story of watching a special on public television 30 years ago. The program took a look at where life on planet Earth came from. After a couple of hours of working backward, using Darwinian evolution as the basis for understanding where we came from, the scientist came down to the most basic form of life – the cell. The cell is pretty much universally agreed to be the basic structural and functional unit of all known living organisms. It is the smallest unit of life that is classified as a living thing and is often called the "building block of life."

Even if you bought into the theory of evolution presented in the PBS show, there was still one major problem with how the program ended: It failed to say where that one living cell came from. And a fundamental law of science is that you cannot get life from non-life.

---

*   Book available at **https://crossexamined.org/**

Whether someone believes in the God of the Bible is one thing, and perhaps agnosticism is understandable. I can have respect for someone who genuinely says, "I don't know if God exists, but I am willing to consider the possibility and look at the evidence." But for someone to just be an outright atheist – that is, to declare with certainty that there is no God – doesn't seem intellectually plausible when you consider the marvel that is the world around us.

In fact, the Bible – in Psalm 53:1 – is more direct. It reads: "*The fool has said in his heart, 'There is no God.'*"

Charles Darwin, often called the "Father of Evolution," is best known for his work titled *The Origin of Species*. In Chapter 6 of that book, he goes into great detail about the human eye. He writes:

> *To suppose that the eye, with all its inimitable contrivances for adjusting the focus to different distances, for admitting different amounts of light, and for the correction of spherical and chromatic aberration, could have been formed by natural selection [evolution], seems, I freely confess, absurd in the highest possible degree.*

Darwin then goes on to basically say, "But it could happen." In other words, Darwin says it's absurd to believe that the eye could have been formed by evolution, but he believes it was anyway. You can read that part for yourself if you wish, but it is painful to read because it is a tortured attempt to explain away what he had just admitted was "absurd in the highest possible degree."

Renowned scientist Albert Einstein, named Person of the Century by *Time* magazine in 1999, was an agnostic. He did not believe in a personal God. However, he did say this: "Everyone who is seriously involved in the pursuit of science becomes convinced that a spirit is manifest in the laws of the universe – a spirit vastly superior to man, and one in the face of which our modest powers must feel humble."

I believe God created the heavens and the earth. And unlike Mr. Einstein, I *do* believe in a personal God, which is what Jesus Christ taught. The New Testament teaches that Jesus is the one and only mediator between God and man. That is to say that man cannot reach God without going through Jesus Christ. You can choose not to believe that, but it is the essential doctrine of the New Testament.

Jesus Himself said in John 3:16-17, *"For God so loved the world, that He gave His only begotten Son, that whoever believes in Him shall not perish, but have eternal life. For God did not send the Son into the world to judge the world, but that the world might be saved through Him."*

FOR GOD SO LOVED ...

November 2012 – My dad was a United Methodist pastor when I was young. Like many of you reading this, I learned many Bible stories as a child. Many nights Dad would read to his four children about Daniel, Moses, David, Peter, and Jesus. I still have all those Bible story books, which contain individual stories and sketches.

I went to Sunday School every week, Camp Lake Stephens church camp and Vacation Bible School in the summer, and home Bible studies weekly as a teen. My lovely and talented wife Alison and I have always had as a priority that the church we attend must stress the teaching of God's Word. In short, the Bible has been a big part of my life for nearly five decades now.

When you grow up steeped in something, you just naturally assume it to be true – whatever it is. It wasn't until my college years that I began to hear some people openly challenge the veracity of the Bible.

I remember my anatomy and physiology professor at Mississippi State University speaking of Darwinian evolution as a fact, not a theory. That made such an impression on me that I remember it like it was yesterday.

Then I met some fellow students who would openly question the Bible. When they would do so, I would stand back and wait for the lightning bolt to strike them dead. It never did. Looking back, I realize that was good for me. It's good to have your assumptions about anything challenged. It makes you examine what you believe.

Since those college years, I've read many books on what is called "biblical apologetics." There is a lot you can say about the Bible that is logical, understandable, historical, and verifiable – for instance, many places mentioned in the Scriptures are still in existence today ... Jerusalem and Egypt, for example. But then there is a lot that is mysterious and unexplained – sometimes even seemingly cruel or contradictory, although most of these "contradictions" can be explained with a closer study of the text. The Bible is both simple and complex.

But one of the most compelling reasons to believe the Bible is true is the fact that we still have an ethnic group of people called "Jews." (In the Bible, the Jews are also referred to as "Hebrews" or "Israelites.")

There are many groups of people also mentioned in the Bible that have long since passed from the face of the earth. But the Jews have remained. God selected the Jews to be His "chosen people," beginning with Abraham. In other words, God discriminated in favor of the Jews. Why? Because He wanted to, and God can do whatever He wants.

When Jesus Christ came to Earth, He opened up God's favor to anyone who would follow Him – not just the Jews. There is a reason John 3:16 is the most well-known verse in the Bible. It expresses this idea of a universal invitation for salvation – perhaps better than any other verse: "*For God so loved the world, that He gave His only begotten Son, that whoever believes in Him shall not perish, but have eternal life.*"

I believe it takes great faith to believe that the Bible was written solely by mere men. The **chance** of 66 books … penned over a 1,600-year period … by 40 men in the ancient world … all coming together into one volume – that is remarkable in itself … even if you believe in chance.

But more amazing is the majesty, scope, and consistency of all parts of the Bible. A fair reading has to suggest to any reasonable person that it's more than just a book. And it is. For it showed me my sin and the glorious God Who, at great cost to Himself, provided a remedy for it. And for that, I am eternally grateful.

TO JUDGE OR NOT TO JUDGE ...
THAT IS THE QUESTION

April 2013 – Do you know the favorite Bible verse of those who don't believe in the Bible's authority? Think about it. It's not hard. The favorite Bible verse of those who do not believe in the Bible is: *"Do not judge so that you will not be judged"* (Matthew 7:1).

Now these folks cannot tell you where this verse is in the Bible because they don't read it. But they have heard it is in the Scriptures somewhere, so if they don't like something you say when you pronounce something to be right or wrong, they whip out Matthew 7:1, and that is supposed to be the end of the discussion.

One of the problems is, if you tell someone he has no right to judge someone else, you have thereby judged him for judging. You have done precisely what you claim to be against – judging. That makes you a hypocrite. But that then begs the question, "Why is it wrong to be a hypocrite?" Who made that judgment? We just assume that to be a true statement, which is a presupposition. But presuppositions need a foundation to be authoritative.

For example, the teachings of Jesus Christ are authoritative for those who believe He is the Son of God.

Each one of us has a worldview on which we base our lives – presuppositions we operate under and make decisions on. Because of our country's Christian heritage, most Americans, either consciously or subconsciously, derive their presuppositions about life and morality from the Bible. Ask an average man on the street if lying is right or wrong behavior, and he is going to tell you it's wrong. Ask who decided lying was wrong, and he will either say, "It just is," or "My parents taught me it was wrong" or "The Bible says so."

However, "It just is" is not an answer to the question; it is an opinion. Neither is "My parents taught me." Parents are authority figures, but they do not define morality in any absolute way because they are humans whose opinions are subject to change. "The Bible says so," is a legitimate answer because if you believe the Bible is God's Word, then you want to obey God so you don't fall into disfavor with a Supreme Being Who can control your eternal destiny.

A lot of Americans will say they subscribe to the idea that a person should be free to do whatever he wishes "as long as it does not hurt anyone else." This view, again, is based on the presuppositions that freedom is "good," and it is morally "wrong" to hurt someone else. Who made these rules? Who says freedom is morally superior to bondage? And why is it wrong to hurt someone else? Who says?

To injure or hurt someone else goes against biblical teaching. That is where the idea that it is wrong to hurt someone comes from in the first place. The Golden Rule was given to us by Jesus Christ.

Other cultures in the world, such as communist countries, use the atheistic state government as the agent for defining what is right or wrong behavior. It's called "totalitarianism" for a reason. In Muslim countries, Islamic law and teaching dominates the people's behavior. They define good and evil ... right and wrong. Most European countries have what's left of their Christian heritage to guide them, although the continent today is mostly secular, with Islam rising as a possible replacement to secularism in the coming decades.

It is a healthy exercise to ask ourselves where we get the moral values that govern our lives. Is it each person for himself, or do we acknowledge a higher power with authority to declare such?

God calls on all men to submit to His will and authority. Let us pray that America will become a God-fearing nation again. In Matthew 10:28, Jesus declared: *"Do not fear those who kill the body but are unable to kill the soul; but rather fear Him who is able to destroy both soul and body in hell."*

WORLDVIEWS AND MORALITY

May 2013 – Everyone has a worldview – admit it or not. Yes, you have one, too. We all have a mindset through which we see the world and determine what is right and wrong, good and evil, moral and immoral.

Generally speaking, a person's religious persuasion (or lack thereof) seems to have the most profound impact on his or her worldview. One example of this is the annual story about Mississippi being among the poorest states and among the most charitable states at the same time. That does not make much sense unless you factor in religion. The reason for this is that Mississippi has the nation's highest percentage of church attendance, and the church teaches that God expects his followers to put some of their income into the offering plate to advance Christianity here and abroad.

A growing percentage of Americans are defining themselves as "spiritual," rather than "Christian" or "religious." Being atheistic or agnostic does not really appeal to most Americans because to believe in nothing seems void and meaningless, and Americans don't like hopelessness. But by being ambiguously "spiritual," a person is able to define "god" in his own terms, which can evolve with the individual's interests, wants, needs, or desires.

Neither does a "spiritual" person have to answer to a "god" for anything. There are no rules to follow as with traditional religious teaching. The rules are whatever you want them to be – if any at all. This approach to "religion" appeals to the selfish nature of man, who does not want to be told by anyone or any being that they must conform their lives to some fixed standards of behavior or suffer consequences.

The holy book of Christianity is, of course, the Bible. It is there for all to read and scrutinize. Even Christians disagree on how to apply and interpret some Scriptures. You can intellectually rip it to shreds, but at least it is written down in black and white so each person can decide for himself if he finds it credible or not.

With atheism, there is no similar document to scrutinize or criticize because there is nothing to believe in. And as we have said, with "spirituality," it can mean anything and everything under the sun, so here again, there is no doctrine that can be held up to scrutiny as an unbeliever might do with the Bible. That gives the atheist, the agnostic, and the spiritualist the justification to attack the Bible without ever having to defend their own belief systems ... because they don't have any to defend.

But this does beg the question for the person who believes this life is all there is: If you believe the Bible's story is bogus, why spend your limited time of existence attacking that which isn't even real? Why care if others want to be what you would call "superstitious"? And if no absolute truth exists, are we not all just left with our own opinions? And what makes one man's opinion morally superior to another man's if there is no higher standard by which to judge opinions?

This leads us back to values and morality. There is personal morality, and there is public morality (which is otherwise known as law). Sometimes the two overlap, but not always.

You may have heard the expression "You can't legislate morality." But the very purpose of law is to impose on all of us a collective moral order to uphold civilization, and Americans have consented that civilization is something they want. Lawmakers decide what is good and bad, right and wrong, acceptable and unacceptable behavior (morality), and then the police and courts enforce these laws.

So morality *can* be legislated; it happens every day. The only question is, whose morality will we choose to turn into law?

WHAT HAPPENED TO REPENTANCE?

From that time Jesus began to preach and say, "Repent, for the kingdom of heaven is at hand."

– Matthew 4:17

January 2014 – I recently heard a very popular Christian speaker talk to a large audience for an hour. He said nothing heretical. He said nothing controversial. He just focused on the "unconditional" love of God. Again, nothing wrong with what he did say, but it is what he did *not* say that bothered me. He said nothing about repentance from sin.

There is a reason Jesus said what he said in the above Bible verse. And there is a reason John the Baptist introduced Jesus to the world with the exact same proclamation in Matthew 3:2: *"Repent, for the kingdom of heaven is at hand."*

There is a popular trend going on in the American Christian church. The trend is to talk of the love of God without talking about the justice of God. But if you read the Bible, it is clear: There exist both the grace of God and the wrath of God, and Jesus Christ spoke of both.

After recently watching Rev. Billy Graham's latest message to America, which was a call for individuals to turn from their sin and follow Jesus Christ, I commented to someone that Dr. Graham would not fill stadiums today with that message as he did for so many decades.

Today's most popular "evangelists" are those who tell people what God can do for them in terms of self-esteem, a better job, whiter teeth, etc. I'm not saying God doesn't bless people with these temporal things of life sometimes. I *am* saying that those things have nothing to do with the fundamentals and essentials of the Christian faith. The attempt is to try and attract people with the potential benefits of a relationship with God rather than attract them with what God requires of them, such as righteousness, holiness, self-denial, sacrifice, etc. (Try selling books with those words on the cover and see if Oprah Winfrey calls you for an interview.)

It is true that God's love for mankind is unconditional. However, in order for man to be in right relationship with God, man must conform his life to match with God's requirement of man. And God does not force this decision on man. God draws a person to himself, but it is the free will of the individual to decide if he or she will obey God's requirements for a right relationship.

Jesus called this experience being "born again." In other words, a person (every human) must understand that he or she has violated God's laws and is forever separated from God spiritually unless he or she repents of sin and trusts in the shed blood of

Jesus on the cross for forgiveness of that sin in order to be counted among those who have been redeemed ... redeemed from the consequences of unrepentant sin, which is death and hell.

What I am writing here is not popular in contemporary America, where we want to live our own lives without interference from God. It's our natural tendency to live for ourselves instead of obeying the commands of God. That is the ongoing struggle between flesh and spirit.

In order to demonstrate our love for Christ, He says we must deny ourselves, pick up our cross daily, and follow Him. Our "cross" is a challenge to wake up daily and try our best to live like Jesus. The way we learn to live like Jesus is to study the Bible, take time to pray, and fellowship with other believers (which we call "church").

God knows we will fail at this, precisely *because* we are human. Sometimes we are tempted by sin, and we give in to it. But the Bible also says that if we confess our sins to God, He is willing to forgive us. That is great news!

No one is compelled to believe this. You may read this and call it foolishness. That is your right. But if that is your view, I challenge you to read one book in the Bible, the Gospel of John, and consider the claims of the Bible and Christ before you dismiss Christianity.

WHEN THE FIGHT COMES TO YOU

February 2014 – There is a difference between going looking for a fight and having a fight come to you. It was that way with the colonists who decided to break away from the king of England in the 1700s. Those soon-to-be Americans – the men and women who founded our country – decided they had had enough abuse from the king, so they made their grievances public with the signing of the Declaration of Independence on July 4, 1776, and the war for America began.

Our founders didn't go looking for a fight with the British crown, but the provocation for a fight came to them. It is much the same way for those of us who believe in traditional Christian values in modern-day America. For the past four decades, we haven't been looking for a fight, but our beliefs and morals have been under assault. For example:

- Honoring God and prayer were very much a part of public life, but then the secularists went against those practices through the courts, and many of us felt the need to fight back by forming Christian legal organizations to challenge the atheists and secularists in the courtrooms.

- Christian teaching regarding sexual behavior was the standard before Alfred Kinsey, Hugh Hefner, and the entertainment industry (Hollywood) began to attack it relentlessly. Television programming from the 1970s forward has proclaimed there are no rules with respect to sex. Christians saw this as having dire consequences for the long-term health of our society and decided to fight back, and we were mocked for doing so.

- The taking of innocent human life through abortion was illegal in most states until the 1973 *Roe v Wade* Supreme Court decision overruled the states and made abortion the law of the land. Some Christians decided to fight back, and thus was born the pro-life movement.

- For all of human history, the definition of marriage has been the union of one man and one woman. The vast majority of states, even liberal California, have reaffirmed this view of marriage in the last 20 years. But one federal judge overruled seven million Californians, and later the Supreme Court concurred, thus changing the legal definition of marriage to include men "marrying" men and women "marrying" women. Talk about a classic oxymoron! Some Christians decided to fight back, and what America will do with this issue remains to be seen.

There are many more examples of what the "culture war" is all about, but I've just laid out four of the more high-profile issues of our time. These issues were why my dad, Rev. Don Wildmon, founded the American Family Association. He saw the need to give Christians (and others who support traditional values) an organized response to the attacks on the Christian value system. That was in 1977. But we have been backed into a corner and left with no recourse but to fight for our values.

There have been other groups like AFA who have also engaged in the effort to preserve and restore these values. The culture war is really a spiritual war; therefore, it is eternal. There will always be good and evil, right and wrong, moral and immoral. And just as these values matter in our personal lives, they also matter for the well-being of our country. If we as a nation continue to rebel against God and godly principles, He will either destroy us or allow us to implode. I can't tell you exactly what that looks like, but judging by historical and biblical accounts, it will be really, really bad.

If you are a Christian soldier, let me encourage, warn, and challenge you:

- Let me encourage you that standing for the Lord and His righteousness is always the right thing to do. We must do what we can, while we can. Elections matter. Building strong families matters. Being involved in your community matters. Winning converts to Christianity matters.

- Let me warn you that the world is against us – and sometimes hostile toward us – because we make moral judgments based on Scripture and proclaim them publicly. Jesus told us this would be the case.

- Finally, let me challenge you to stay involved with groups like AFA. We will win some and we will lose some. But we can't quit. We can never give up.

What a future America will look like for our children, our grandchildren, and Christians in general, is very much at stake.

ONE CHEESEBURGER — HOLD THE CHEESE

March 2014 – "Yes ma'am," I said into the sign with all the pictures of colorful food on it. "I would like a burger, plain – just meat and bread – and a Sprite."

"You want a cheeseburger with what on it, sir?" said the voice back to me.

"No, I don't want a cheeseburger. I want a plain burger with meat and bread only."

I was ordering for my 12-year-old son, Wesley. (I actually like my burgers dressed.) There was a short silence. Then she returned.

"So you want a cheeseburger with pickles only and a Sprite. Would you like some fries to go with that?"

I put my head on the steering wheel in frustration and then went for one more attempt. Deep breath.

"No, I don't want any fries. Listen to me closely. I want a plain burger, just meat and bread. That's it, meat and bread. Now, can you repeat back to me what I just ordered, please?"

She thought about it. A few seconds later, she responded, "So you want a cheeseburger without cheese?"

Classic.

For me to say anything sarcastic at this point would have only confused things further, so I restrained myself. I looked at my three kids. They were dying laughing by this time.

"That's right, ma'am. You call it whatever you want to call it," I said, trying not to laugh. "I just want a piece of meat between a top bun and a bottom bun and nothing else."

When I got to the window, she said she was sorry, it had been a long day. I told her it was the first time I had had a hamburger referred to as "a cheeseburger without cheese." We both laughed.

Everyone should have to work in the fast-food business for at least a few months. You grow as a person. I know I did.

In fact, if you came by Burger King on South Gloster in Tupelo, Mississippi, during the summer of 1980, I would have likely had a hand in getting your Whopper, fries, and drink out to you. But there is no way for me to know if you were at the front counter or at the drive-thru window because my boss kept me in the back, away from customers. I wasn't the sharpest knife in the drawer back then, so I worked in the kitchen.

I was a little slow at first because Mama had always made my burgers for me, but by the end of the summer, I could work the fry basket, operate the drink machine, and run the burger line. I was an interchangeable drill bit – a multi-talented, smooth operator.

Still, sometimes, I would peer out the small rectangular window where we, the lowly burger-makers, fry-dippers, and drink-fillers, would place your order when it was ready. I wondered what it must feel like to work the front counter and deal with the friendly, hungry faces of real people. That was a job my boss mostly assigned to the cute, perky, smiling girls. The dull teenage boys like me were sentenced to duties away from the public.

"Wildmon, what are you staring at? Get me that Whopper with cheese now!" was something I heard from the other side of the small rectangular window more than once that summer.

Sometimes I would daydream. Did you ever do that as a teenager?

What's so appealing about a fast-food restaurant with a drive-thru window is not only the colorful pictures of tasty food, but also the fact that we can pick and choose what we want and how we want it fixed, and then get it to go. Gulp it down on the run. Kind of like the American version of Christianity these days. Have you noticed?

So many of us treat our relationship with the Lord the same way we order fast food. "Lord, gimme a little of this, some of that, and bless it if you would. Amen."

Consistency and valued time with the Lord are what I desire more of. It's been a challenge for me, spending quality time in devotion, prayer, and worship. I often think I can get by on spiritual fast food, when Jesus says He wants me to come dine at His table of bounty and blessing.

Well, I worked my one summer at a fast-food place. That was all I needed. I grew up some. Learned how to treat grease burns. Learned how to fill a Diet Pepsi and a Mountain Dew at the same time. (It's not as easy as you think.) I never did, however, learn to make a cheeseburger without cheese.

GOD'S WISDOM THROUGH SOLOMON

January 2015 – Do yourself a favor – put away your cell phone or other gadget and get out a Bible. Turn to the book of Proverbs. If you are like me, you will find these words of wisdom addictive. You read one, and it's so good, you want to read another and another.

Here are some nuggets from the book of Proverbs. They were likely written nearly 1,000 years before the birth of Jesus Christ. Many are profound and pointed. Some are funny. And some make you wonder, "How did this make it in here?" (I understand that these verses are included in the Old Testament because God put them there, so please don't email me.) Here are a few of my favorites:

- *The fear of the Lord is the beginning of knowledge (1:7a).*

- *Trust in the Lord with all your heart / And do not lean on your own understanding. / In all your ways acknowledge Him, / And He will make your paths straight (3:5-6).*

- *Poor is he who works with a negligent hand, / But the hand of the diligent makes rich (10:4).*

- *When pride comes, then comes dishonor, / But with the humble is wisdom (11:2).*

- *Riches do not profit in the day of wrath, / But righteousness delivers from death (11:4).*

- *The generous man will be prosperous, / And he who waters will himself be watered (11:25).*

- *There is one who speaks rashly like the thrusts of a sword, / But the tongue of the wise brings healing (12:18).*

- *Anxiety in a man's heart weighs it down, / But a good word makes it glad (12:25).*

- *The way of a fool is right in his own eyes, / But a wise man is he who listens to counsel (12:15).*

- *A wise man is cautious and turns away from evil, / But a fool is arrogant and careless (14:16).*

- *Leave the presence of a fool, / Or you will not discern words of knowledge (14:7).*

- *He who is slow to anger has great understanding, / But he who is quick-tempered exalts folly (14:29).*

- *Righteousness exalts a nation, / But sin is a disgrace to any people (14:34).*

- *A gentle answer turns away wrath, / But a harsh word stirs up anger (15:1).*

- *The eyes of the Lord are in every place, / Watching the evil and the good (15:3).*

- *A joyful heart makes a cheerful face, / But when the heart is sad, the spirit is broken (15:13).*

- *Better is a little with the fear of the Lord / Than great treasure and turmoil with it (15:16).*

- *Pride goes before destruction, / And a haughty spirit before stumbling (16:18).*

- *A perverse man spreads strife, / And a slanderer separates intimate friends (16:28).*

- *Grandchildren are the crown of old men, / And the glory of sons is their fathers (17:6).*

- *A joyful heart is good medicine (17:22a).*

- *He who restrains his words has knowledge, / And he who has a cool spirit is a man of understanding (17:27).*

- *Death and life are in the power of the tongue (18:21a).*

- *The spirit of man is the lamp of the Lord, / Searching all the innermost parts of his being (20:27).*

- *The plans of the diligent lead surely to advantage, / But everyone who is hasty comes surely to poverty (21:5).*

- *It is better to live in a desert land / Than with a contentious and vexing woman (21:19).*

- *A good name is to be more desired than great wealth, / Favor is better than silver and gold. (22:1).*

- *Do not associate with a man given to anger; / Or go with a hot-tempered man (22:24).*

- *Do not hold back discipline from the child, / Although you strike him with the rod, he will not die. / You shall strike him with the rod / And rescue his soul from Sheol (23:13-14).*

- *Like one who takes a dog by the ears / Is he who passes by and meddles with strife not belonging to him (26:17).*

- *He who blesses his friend with a loud voice early in the morning, / It will be reckoned a curse to him (27:14).*

- *Iron sharpens iron, / So one man sharpens another (27:17).*

- *As in water face reflects face, / So the heart of man reflects man (27:19).*

- *How blessed is the man who fears always, / But he who hardens his heart will fall into calamity. (28:14).*

- *A fool always loses his temper, / But a wise man holds it back (29:11).*

- *An excellent wife, who can find? / For her worth is far above jewels (31:10).*

The wisdom of God's Word – no better way to enter the brand-new year.

THE GREATEST GIFT

December 2016 – I had been watching this guy for, I guess, about two years. Almost every time my wife Alison went to Wal-Mart, he was there. And almost every time Alison goes to Wal-Mart, I stay in the van and park close to the front of the store. Saves us the trouble of finding a real parking place – and saves me the trouble of having to go in and pretend to enjoy something I personally loathe.

Nothing against the fine folks at Wal-Mart; it's just that I am not a shopper, not even for the bare necessities. I don't even know what brand of shampoo we use. All I know is that it's always there.

But back to the guy in the parking lot … the one who gathers the buggies from all over the lot, lines them up, and pushes them – 50 at a time sometimes – back up to the store. Talk about a thankless job. I don't know what these guys get paid, but it should be above average. No matter what the weather, they must retrieve the buggies.

I have observed him in the hot mugginess of a Mississippi August as I sat in my air-conditioned van. I have watched him as my windshield wipers worked overtime during a hard April shower. And he has gained my respect as I sat inside my warm van on a cold, January night when the wind cut like a knife. The guy is a rock, I've thought many times. I don't exactly know why this fellow and his work captured my attention the way they did. I suppose it was because I knew if I were out there, I would have quit a long time ago.

And I have worked hard manual labor before, my friends, so don't think me a complete office wimp. Worked a summer, while I was in college, for a metal chair manufacturer. They put me to work stacking sets of five boxed metal chairs on wooden pallets … for eight hours a day. First day I almost died. Seriously. I went straight home and went to bed. It was then I knew what a mule's life was about: pain … both mental and physical. It would have been emotional as well, but I was too tired for emotions. But I went back the next day. And then another. And finally the summer was over, and I returned to college with a new appreciation for making a living with my head rather than my back.

Last December I decided that, after admiring the man in the Wal-Mart parking lot for two years, it was time I met him. One day when Alison came back to the van, I pointed him out to her and told her I wanted to do something for him for Christmas. She agreed it was a good idea, so we went over to the Christian bookstore and purchased a really nice Bible and a card. (Yeah, I broke down and went shopping.)

A couple of days later, we were at Wal-Mart again and – as always – there he was. I had the gift with me, and Alison was inside the store, so I just walked up to him and said, "Excuse me, how are you?"

"Fine," he said. "Can I help you?"

"My name's Tim Wildmon and you are …?"

"Ed Jones," he answered.*

"Well, Ed …"

"Say, are you kin to Brother Don Wildmon?"

"Well, yeah, Ed, I am. He's my dad. Why?" (I never know what kind of reaction I'm going to get to this.)

"Oh, I listen to his radio station some. Really enjoy it."

"So, you are a Christian?" I asked.

"Yes, I am," Ed replied.

"Well, Ed, I come here a lot and I've been watching your work, and I just wanted to say I appreciate what you do, and I want to give you a little something for Christmas."

Ed unwrapped the box and opened it to find the Bible. A smile came to his face. He thanked me and said he needed a new one. He told me some about himself and where he went to church. I also told him to open the card later, that I had given him a little something to go to dinner on. We shook hands, I told him that God loved him and to have a merry Christmas, and back to work he went. And to the comfortable van went I.

That gave me a great feeling that day. Inside that Bible I gave Ed can be found a story of the greatest gift of all time. The gift God gave to Ed, to me, and to all who would receive by faith the gift of His Son, Jesus Christ. Take time to read and reread the story.

---

*   Name changed.

HAPPY MOTHER'S DAY

May 2017 – You ever wonder why God gave us only 10 commandments? I say "only" because that doesn't seem like a lot of rules to follow. But then again, because we are so apt to disobey God, we tend to violate these 10.

It shouldn't be that way. It doesn't have to be that way, but I'm going on personal experience and what I know to be true from others. Our goal each day should be to live as God has taught in the Ten Commandments and the Sermon on the Mount.

In Exodus 20:12, we find the fifth commandment: *"Honor your father and your mother, that your days may be prolonged in the land which the Lord your God gives you."*

Now the Ten Commandments were given to the children of Israel, but because they are reconfirmed in the New Testament, it means that they apply to Christians today as well. So believers are to "honor" their parents. For most of you reading this, you don't have a problem with this because you have had a good relationship with your parents. However, for others who have had an alcoholic father or a drug-addicted mother, it may not be so easy.

The best way I can answer this is to use the presidency as an example. I didn't agree with much of anything President Obama did in office, but I still had respect for the office of the presidency. I see this commandment in the same way. We are to hold in high esteem the "office" of mother.

I certainly find this easy to do with my mom. Lynda Lou Bennett was born June 23, 1940, in Booneville, Mississippi. Like many of that generation, she was raised on a farm. In Mom's case, she grew up with three younger siblings in the rolling hills of Tishomingo County in the northeast corner of the state.

In high school and college, mom was a beauty queen, a basketball star (who once scored 54 points in a game), and a top scholar.

One summer she attended Blue Mountain College in nearby Blue Mountain, Mississippi, where she met a young man named Don Wildmon, who asked her out for a date. She declined, saying she had to study for a chemistry class. He asked her a second time, and she declined; she had to get her hair done. Fortunately for me, Don swallowed his pride and asked her out a third time, and finally she said yes. They went to a movie, and on the way back to the dorm, Don told Lynda he was going to marry her. That's right – on their first date. Dad was ambitious like that and almost always got what he went after.

I was the first of four children Mom had from 1963 to 1971. She served Dad faithfully as a pastor's wife – even though she couldn't play the piano. (I don't know about where you're from, but a pastor has a lot better chance of getting a pulpit in a little Southern church if his wife plays the piano.)

She taught junior high home economics after we all reached school age, and she taught cake decorating classes on the side to help make ends meet. Like any good mother, she invested herself into teaching her four children right from wrong and how to get the most out of life. If she has ever sinned, I don't think anyone knows about it. She was – and is still today – a traditional, mannered, sweet, loving, praying, caring Southern belle. In short, she is a godly, Proverbs 31 woman.

We need to do as the Bible says and honor our mothers. Jesus certainly did. There is an old saying: The hand that rocks the cradle rules the world.

How true that saying is. How true it is.

Thanks for all you've done for me, Mom. Happy Mother's Day!

FOUR DECADES OF TRUSTING GOD

When we walk with the Lord
In the light of His Word,
What a glory He sheds on our way;
While we do His good will,
He abides with us still,
And with all who will trust and obey.

> – From the hymn "Trust and Obey"
> (lyrics by John Henry Sammis)

July-August 2017 – I was 14 years old when my dad, Don Wildmon, started the National Federation for Decency, which later became American Family Association. The year was 1977. What kicked it all off was when Dad asked the congregation he pastored at First United Methodist Church in Southaven, Mississippi, to participate in "Turn the Television Off Week."

The local news media in Memphis found out about it, then the story hit the wire, and media calls from across the country started pouring in to the pastor's office. The church secretary was used to answering questions about what time services started and when the next potluck supper was scheduled. Now she was getting calls from NBC News and Wall Street Journal. In today's vernacular, we would say the story of a small-town preacher protesting sex, violence, and profanity on television "went viral."

It was in the mid-1970s and early 1980s that God began to raise up several Christian leaders to address the decline of morality and common decency in America. They came from different denominations and varied backgrounds. Names that come to mind include D. James Kennedy, Jerry Falwell, James Dobson, Tim and Beverly LaHaye, Phyllis Schlafly, Larry Burkett, Marlon Maddox, Adrian Rogers, and Pat Robertson. Of course, there were many others.

Politically, this group of leaders and the millions of people they represented became known as the "religious right." That term was meant to be pejorative when used by the liberal media, but it was basically that group of people who put Ronald Reagan in the White House in 1980 with a stunning victory over incumbent Jimmy Carter.

In the 1980s, Dad was making regular appearances on national television news shows like **Nightline** with Ted Koppel and **Tomorrow** with the late Tom Snyder. I remember when I was in high school traveling to Washington, D.C., so Dad could appear on the **McNeal/Lehrer Report** on PBS and NBC's **Meet the Press**. At the time, those programs were leading news sources, so Dad's profile and that of AFA began to rise across the country.

If I had to name one issue that put AFA on the national map and that brought in many new members to our cause, it was when the movie **The Last Temptation of Christ** was released in 1988. This was a blasphemous film about Christ directed by famed Hollywood liberal Martin Scorsese. I remember we had about 10 employees at the time, and we would all sit and take hundreds of phone calls a day from people all over America who wanted copies of our petition to theaters asking that they not show this movie. It worked. The movie only made it to 1% of the theaters in the country and was a financial flop.

If you ask our supporters what one word describes why they support AFA, the word would likely be "action." AFA addresses the moral issues of our day and attempts to bring about change in favor of the Christian teaching of right and wrong. So we take on specific issues on a weekly basis. However, we are also about framing the worldview conflict between Christianity and secular humanism (progressivism) that is greater than any one issue. And we take action by educating the Christian community.

The mission of AFA is not hard to understand. Whatever God is for, we are for, and whatever God is against, we are against. That's not our official mission statement, but it simplifies the reason we do what we do. And where do we get our guidance on what God is for and against? From the Bible.

I am encouraged by people like you who believe in that mission and who continue to stand in obedience to God, for the love of our country. It is only respect for Christian values that will restore our nation's crumbling moral foundation.

Today is another opportunity for us to stand for those values as we go forward together practicing our trust in our great God.

THE TRUTH IS STILL THE TRUTH

December 2018 – The Christmas season has always held a special place in the hearts of most Americans. It still does with millions of us, but it's hard to tell sometimes with all the political correctness sweeping our land. We Christians are told we might offend non-Christians if we talk about Christmas too much.

It's ironic to watch some of these companies depend on the Christmas gift-giving season to make it into the black, then intentionally avoid any mention of that very holiday that makes their company profitable. I'm glad to say American Family Association has brought attention to this issue, and we have heard from many companies that agree with us and have returned to allowing the word "Christmas" to be used in their advertising and store promotions.

The Hollywood crowd and liberal elites want to push us into a generic "holiday" celebration. Many people have also succumbed to multiculturalism, which basically contends that all cultures are morally equal, so – again – to raise Christmas over other religious holidays would offend other cultures. It's a shame what the politically correct crowd has tried to do with Christmas in our country. Some may say this really doesn't matter, but it's all part of the move by the secular left to de-Christianize America.

My growing-up years were in the 1960s and 1970s. There were so many wonderful Christmas specials on television in late November and through December: Andy Williams, Perry Como, Bob Hope, and more.

And then there were the animated specials our family also made it a point to watch every year, including **A Charlie Brown Christmas**, which first aired in 1965 and continues on network television today. Through the lovable cartoon characters from the **Peanuts** cartoon series, the reason for Christmas is presented in the school play when Linus tells Charlie Brown he knows the real reason for Christmas and goes on stage in front of the spotlight and quotes from the book of Luke:

> *"And there were in the same country shepherds abiding in the field, keeping watch over their flock by night. And, lo, the angel of the Lord came upon them, and the glory of the Lord shone round about them: and they were sore afraid. And the angel said unto them, Fear not: for, behold, I bring you tidings of great joy, which shall be to all people. For unto you is born this day in the city of David a Savior, which is Christ the Lord. And this shall be a sign unto you; Ye shall find the babe wrapped in swaddling clothes, lying in a manger. And suddenly there was with the angel a multitude of the heavenly host praising God, and saying, Glory to God in the highest, and on earth peace, goodwill toward men."*

Then Linus concludes with the truth: "That's what Christmas is all about, Charlie Brown."

Kudos to the late Charles Shultz, creator of Peanuts, for making this the main point of **A Charlie Brown Christmas**. There is no way a show that quoted that much Bible could ever make it onto network television today if it were not already an entrenched and established tradition.

As Christians we need to continue to use the Christmas season to share with the world around us the real reason for the celebration. That's why AFA promotes our Christmas buttons and wristbands each year. We have distributed millions of these in the last few years.

Keeping the Christmas season alive in our popular culture causes a lot of people to think about the reason for the season. This is a good thing. That's exactly why so many on the left want to get rid of it.

Let's keep Christmas in America, and let's keep Christ in Christmas.

IF THE WORLD HATES YOU, REMEMBER ...

January-February 2019 – Do you ever wonder why so many people in the world hate Christians? Have you ever wondered why some governments – China, for example – do not want Christianity in their land? What is it about following Jesus that causes such hostility?

Christians possess no physical army that would pose a military threat. Christianity does not teach force or violence as a way of spreading its message. Ironically, most people in the world who despise Christianity don't even believe God exists. So why are they so passionate in their opposition to a God they don't believe exists?

In John 15:18-25, Jesus spoke about this:

> *"If the world hates you, you know that it has hated Me before it hated you. If you were of the world, the world would love its own; but because you are not of the world, but I chose you out of the world, because of this the world hates you. Remember the word that I said to you, 'A slave is not greater than his master.' If they persecuted Me, they*

will also persecute you; if they kept My word, they will keep yours also. But all these things they will do to you for My name's sake, because they do not know the One who sent Me. If I had not come and spoken to them, they would not have sin, but now they have no excuse for their sin. He who hates Me hates My Father also. If I had not done among them the works which no one else did, they would not have sin; but now they have both seen and hated Me and My Father as well. But they have done this to fulfill the word that is written in their Law, 'They hated Me without a cause.'"

In this passage, Jesus explains why – against all logic – the world hates the followers of Jesus. The reason He gives: It hated Him first, and we are His followers. Simple as that.

If you've been paying attention, you already know that America seems to be witnessing the truth of Jesus' words more and more these days.

You would think that when people hate someone else, they would have reason, like an offense, injury, or jealousy. That certainly happens, but in the case of our society turning on Christians, something deeper is going on.

After all, America was founded on biblical principles and be-came a bastion of liberty and freedom as a result. Yes, I know our nation is not perfect – never was and never will be – but in the flow of history, we're way ahead of every other country. That's why people are desperately storming our southern border to get in.

It makes no sense that many in our nation would destroy the grand ideas that made America the envy of the world. But then, Jesus already said hatred for Him is without reason.

But just because such hatred is not reasonable, that doesn't mean it is without explanation. Remember the context of the Gospel passage above. Jesus' ministry was growing. As it threatened to upend everything in the Jewish religious leaders' world, they conspired with the Romans to have Him killed.

Isn't that essentially the same reason worldly power structures hate Jesus and His followers? Call them communists, socialists, or secular progressives, but Christianity brings the kind of freedom and liberty that undermines their godless rule. And such movements have no tolerance for that.

That's sounding more and more like the America we are living in, isn't it?

So when the followers of Christ stand to say that human life is sacred because we are made in the image of God, can we expect hatred with no reason? Yes, because the world first hated the Creator.

When we say that marriage is between one woman and one man for life, can we expect hatred with no reason? Yes, because it first hated the One Who instituted marriage.

When we challenge the world's view that heterosexuality is just one option among many equal choices regarding healthy human sexuality, can we expect hatred with no reason? Yes, because the world first hated humanity's marvelous designer.

And when we proclaim the incredibly good news that faith in Jesus Christ is the only way sinful men can be reconciled to a Holy God, can we expect unreasonable hatred? Yes. Remember, Jesus proclaimed that Good News. And it got Him killed.

DO THE WORK; DONATIONS WILL FOLLOW

July 2019 – June marked 42 years of ministry for us here at American Family Association. Hard to believe, but it was in the summer of 1977 that my father, Don Wildmon, left the pulpit ministry as a pastor in the United Methodist Church and answered God's call to raise up an army of fellow Americans who saw the moral decline our country was experiencing and wanted to do something about it.

Dad was 39 years old when he started the National Federation for Decency, which later became AFA. You have to understand, when he left the church, he had no steady income. There was no one person or group of people making sure he could feed his family while he got this new ministry off the ground. And there were Mom and four of us children in our home on Greenbrier Drive in Southaven, Mississippi.

In those first few months, Dad had incurred some debt. He was extremely frugal, with his office in our home; but still, postage, phone bills, printing, paper, etc. were necessary to get the word out.

He was once in need of $5,000, and he didn't know where that was going to come from. Then one afternoon, while he was mowing our yard, a gentleman called the house asking for Don Wildmon. Mom went to tell Dad, and he stopped mowing, wiped his brow, and came inside to answer the phone.

As he tells the story, it was a businessman he had heard of but did not know personally. The man was in Dallas at a conference with many conservative and Christian leaders and wanted to know why Dad was not in attendance.

"Well, I don't have any money," Dad told the fellow.

"I understand," the man responded. "What is your address? I'm going to send a check for $5,000 to you today."

That was a specific answer to prayer for Dad. It was more confirmation that he was doing God's will.

A year later, he found himself in the same situation – $5,000 in debt and not knowing where the money was going to come from. Then one afternoon, the phone rang, and it was a Memphis businessman who owned a chain of discount stores across the Southeast. He had read in the newspaper about what Dad was doing and got his number from the phone book.

As the conversation wound down, the man said this to dad: "I am mainly calling to encourage you, brother, and to let you know my wife and I have talked about it and have decided to send you a check for $5,000 today."

God came through again.

After that, I don't think AFA had to borrow money but one time, and that was a loan to construct a building, and that was paid off in a year. Other than that, Dad always operated in the black. Dad was notorious for his frugality and always made sure all the lights were turned off and the air conditioning was adjusted before he locked the doors at the end of the day.

Whatever criticisms may be said of Don Wildmon, wasting money would not be one of them. He often reminded the staff that the backbone of AFA's support was people who were giving sacrificially.

Dad is 81 now and doesn't come into the office much. His body and mind have slowed – it happens to us all if we live long enough. But he asks me about the work we're doing and the issues that we are addressing. Then he often reminds me to manage the ministry money well and not to get into "financial trouble."

He used to get irritated by ministries always begging for money. He used to say to me that if you have to beg for money all the time, you need to go ahead and close the doors. "It's a bad witness," he would say.

Dad stressed to do the work and "treat your supporters like adults." Don't try to manipulate them. "Do the work, and the donations will follow," he would often say as he mentored me for over 30 years here.

Thank you for supporting AFA. Together, we will continue to raise the banner of righteousness across our country for years to come.

HOPE BUILT ON THE SOLID ROCK

October 2019 – One of my favorite words is "hope." The dictionary defines it this way: "grounds for believing something good may happen." I remember as a child watching Oral Roberts on television. He would end each program by saying, "Something good is going to happen to you today!"

My wife Alison and I liked the word so much, we named our firstborn, our daughter, Wriley Hope.

Before every season, sports fans get excited thinking this may be the year their team wins big. We say, "Hope springs eternal," an expression possibly first coined by 18th-century British poet Alexander Pope.

I enjoy golfing, but if I have a bad hole, I've learned not to let it bother me more than a couple of minutes. Why? Because as soon I put my club back in the bag, it's about 60 seconds before my cart arrives at the next tee box – the next opportunity for something good to happen. There is renewed hope that I may make a par.

To go a little deeper, *hope* is also very much a biblical word. One of the most well-known Bible chapters is 1 Corinthians 13, where verse 13 reads: *"And now these three remain: faith, hope, and love. But the greatest of these is love."*

The fact that the Lord would put "hope" in with "faith" and "love" tells me that hope (in a spiritual sense) is much more than what we call "wishful thinking." Like faith and love, hope is a powerful force God puts in the hearts of followers of Jesus Christ to help us maintain a biblical perspective on life and the world around us.

Our work here at AFA is to advance the kingdom of God ... to promote good and oppose evil. We do that by giving leadership to the Christian community in several areas, including politics and government. AFA fights spiritual wickedness every day. In fact, we are often targeted by others for this very reason.

If we look around at what is happening in our country and in the world, it would be easy to despair. There is so much sin and immorality right out in the open today. Fewer Americans are going to church, and sadly, many of our churches are falling into the hands of leaders who compromise with the world. In the broader culture, a growing attitude toward Christians is that we should shut up and stay in our churches.

But Christians can't do that. Why? Because we have hope in a great God! We have hope that He can change lives and save the country we love from destruction. Like many of you reading this, I have children and grandchildren, and I want to see them have the opportunity to live free. I want them to be able to live in a country that values human life. I want them to grow up in a country that respects law and order.

Without a return of reverence for God, tyranny will one day take our country. That's how history works. But we still have hope; we know what God has done for our nation in the past. Revivals have swept the land. In fact, the divine impact of the First and Second Great Awakenings is evident even today.

Sometimes we are accused by fellow Christians of putting our faith in tools of man to bring about change in our government and in our culture. But we understand that while we must do our part as the Bible commands (to live righteously and stand for the Lord), we have hope that no matter where the road leads, God will take care of those who have given their lives to Him. So we trust in the Lord – we have a hope – that no matter what, God reigns now and forever.

That sentiment is captured in the lines from one of my favorite hymns, "The Solid Rock," by Edward Mote:

> *My hope is built on nothing less*
> *Than Jesus' blood and righteousness.*
> *I dare not trust the sweetest frame,*
> *But wholly lean on Jesus' name.*
>
> *On Christ the solid rock I stand,*
> *All other ground is sinking sand;*
> *All other ground is sinking sand.*

I LOOKED UP IN THE BLEACHERS ...
DAD WAS THERE

June 2020 – I have a joke that I believe is original with me and that is this: On Mother's Day at church, we honor the moms with flowers, and the pastor reads Proverbs 31. But on Father's Day, there are no gift cards to the sporting goods store handed out. No, instead the pastor usually takes the whole sermon to preach on "Seven Ways You Can Be a Better Dad."

Why is this?

Can you imagine a Mother's Day sermon titled "Seven Ways Mothers Can Get Their Act Together"? Now that would be funny, to see the faces of the ladies in the congregation when the pastor announced that title!

Father's Day 2020 is June 21. Like millions of Americans, I will be honoring my father on that day.

My dad is Donald Ellis Wildmon. Most people call him Brother Don. Dad was born on January 18, 1938, in Tippah County in the hills of Northeast Mississippi. Like a lot of babies in those times, he was delivered at home. He was sickly as a child, and his mom said she wondered many times if Don would survive his childhood.

Dad said he was called by the Lord to preach when he was 18 years old. He married my mom in March 1961. In 1963, I was their firstborn while Dad was serving two years in the Army at Fort Leonard Wood, Missouri. Don and Lynda Wildmon would have three more children by 1971, when Dad began to fulfill that earlier calling, pastoring Methodist churches in Iuka, Tupelo, and Southaven, Mississippi.

In December 1977, Dad had a one-on-one meeting with God. God told Dad he was to leave the pulpit and birth an organization that would galvanize Christians to fight back against those pushing immorality in our country. So Dad, not knowing exactly what he would face or exactly how to accomplish the mission, founded what was first called the National Federation for Decency and what has been known as American Family Association since 1988.

Some people are given the gift of ideas or visions but are not so gifted at making them happen. And some people have the ability to create, build, and organize. But rare are the people who can both see *what* needs to be done and also have the smarts to know *how* to get it done. And if you combine that with a heart for God, you've got a powerhouse for good. That was my dad. Which only confirms that God knew exactly which servant to assign this task to.

But since we are celebrating Father's Day in June, I wanted to say a few things about Brother Don, my dad.

When he was a young pastor of a newly organized church, he was a very busy man, but he always put his wife and four children first. And like most children, I looked up to my dad, and I wanted to please him. That's how it should be.

When I was a kid, I played baseball. I always knew if my dad was in the stands because I peeked through the dugout before each game. Because of his full schedule, sometimes he didn't make the start of my games, which bothered me some.

But one father-son memory I will always cherish was when I hit my first (and only) home run over the fence in youth baseball. As I rounded the bases and came to home plate to be swarmed by my teammates, I looked up in the bleachers, hoping and praying that Dad was there to see it. And he was! Smiling from ear to ear and fist-pumping for me!

I'll never forget that moment.

Happy Father's Day, Dad!

PROGRESSIVES, POLITICS, POWER, AND PERSECUTION

August 2020 – One day recently, I was thinking about all the turmoil in our country now with seemingly no answers to the problems causing so much division among Americans. Words from a song made famous by the late Andraé Crouch came to me: "Jesus is the answer for the world today. Above Him there's no other, Jesus is the way."

Because we believe the Bible, we followers of Jesus Christ are really the only people who can clearly see what is happening in our country and our world; the Bible says we can see things with "spiritual eyes." The Scripture says there is a spiritual war going on between God and Satan. Tell that to people who don't know Christ, and they look at you as if you have three heads. Or they mock and curse you as a "religious fanatic" or "Jesus freak." But that is to be expected because the world cannot see with spiritual eyes. Only people who have been redeemed and born again can really understand these things.

In fact, we Christians have more in common with our brothers and sisters in the faith than we do with our brothers and sisters by blood, unless they, too, are Christians. That is why we often refer to one another as "brother" or "sister."

There is an intensifying movement to destroy America as we have known it. Secular "progressives" are engaging in an open revolution against our constitutional republic and Christianity. If you don't understand what "progressive" means politically, think Marxism, which is based on atheism. Progressives think Christians are foolish and find us a great impediment to their agenda because of our numbers.

Barack Obama once derided us as people who "cling to guns or religion." Hillary Clinton referred to us as a "basket of deplorables." There are many more examples of very powerful and popular people who have said worse about us. Again, they hold us in great contempt for our beliefs, and we are still a substantial voting bloc.

Why does Satan want to bring down the United States of America? The primary reason for this is that America has historically been responsible for spreading Christianity more than any other country in the world. I am talking about missionaries from the United States. I am talking about the printing and distribution of Bibles. I am talking about new church plants. I am talking about Christian radio across the globe. I am talking about almost all the works of compassion in Third World countries around the globe that are paid for and performed by American Christians.

With respect to the racial tension we see in our country, Satan is using this issue to divide our country even more than ever before. Christianity promotes love and respect for our fellow man. The gospel is for all people, and God is no respecter of persons. That is clear throughout the New Testament. So if you hold others' skin color against them, or if you believe your skin color makes you somehow a superior human being, that is sin according to God. This sin of mistreating someone based on ethnic or tribal identity has plagued mankind for all of human history. This ideology has led to countless millions enslaved and/or killed.

AFA will continue to teach, equip, and call Christians to action through *AFA Journal*, email Action Alerts, American Family Radio, and other means. The majority of our fellow Americans (including many Christians) don't have a true grasp on what is happening behind the curtain on the world stage. It's our job to educate and motivate as many as we can. We need more troops to fight this spiritual war.

Make no mistake – the organized secular progressives want to replace the Christian influence in America with atheism. We stand in their way. If they are successful, it will lead to persecution – at some point, even physical persecution – of conservatives in general and Christians in particular.

DISPENSE WITH DESPAIR;
WALK IN THE WORD

December 2020 – A typical round of golf takes about four hours. The two men (or women) who occupy the golf cart generally know each other very well, and lots of topics come up between Hole 1 and Hole 18. Rarely is there anything said of profound significance, as golfers are typically out on the course to escape matters of profound significance.

But I was out with my good friend Dave, and we were talking about the turmoil in our country, both politically and culturally. I was saying how depressing it is to see how far our beloved America has gotten away from the God of our fathers, when Dave said, "You know we Christians have to remember this: To despair is to sin."

To which I responded, "Why must you talk about my golf game like that?"

I thought about that several days after our golf outing: "Despair is a sin." I even looked up the word in the dictionary. It means "the complete loss or absence of hope." Now, obviously no one wants to fall into despair about life, but I had never heard about it being a sin – meaning it is something that is displeasing to God.

I don't have to tell you what causes us sometimes to get into an attitude of self-pity or negativity. Every day, we all face myriad temptations to give up or develop a sour attitude, which can suck the life out of us and those around us. Sickness, loss of someone close to us, divorce, losing a job, rebellious children, addiction – all can cause despair.

But how do we fight back? One big way is to understand that what Christians know as "spiritual warfare" is what's going on in our souls – that is, in our minds in particular. But when despair comes to our doors, one of the best ways to combat it head-on is to read the Bible. Or listen to the Bible. Or both.

I do both, but I have found listening to the Bible at night not only helps me learn the Scriptures but also helps soothe my mind and spirit.

Specifically, I believe the book of Psalms was preserved for us to help us with our unbelief.

The Bible is the written Word of God. It gives us perspective. A couple of important concepts become clear when reading the Bible. First, God is huge, and we are tiny. And second, God will take care of those who obey and follow him – even if that means ultimately take care of them. *Ultimately* means "in the end," or as my dad used to say, "When it's all been said and when it's all been done."

The same Bible that comforts us also tells us we must try to do something about our plight. In other words, we have to do our part to help ourselves and help those around us, and yes, I believe, help our country.

If the case of America, it would be easy to despair. We have become a nation of mockers and scoffers when it comes to things of God. Here I go to Psalms again. The book opens with, "*How blessed is the man who does not walk in the counsel of the wicked, nor stand in the path of sinners, nor sit in the seat of scoffers!*"

Things look bleak right now. But we Christians must keep doing everything we can do to stand "*for the sake of righteousness,*" as Jesus called it (Matthew 5:10). It's our service to Him.

We must never despair. God is on His heavenly throne, and He will have the final say on planet Earth.

A REBELLIOUS REPUBLIC – CAN BANKRUPTCY BE FAR BEHIND?

October 2021 – America today reminds me of a family-owned business that is about to go bankrupt. The first generation, who founded the business, put in long hours, blood, sweat, and tears to get it off the ground and profitable. The second generation watched the first generation and made the enterprise even stronger and made even more profit. The third generation put in fewer hours and effort but enjoyed the money and the lifestyle that the business provided. The fourth generation knew little about the business except enjoying the fruits of the hard work previous generations had invested into building the company, and now their customer base is in decline, and the product is starting to deteriorate. Then the business goes into bankruptcy and has to close down, all because the fourth generation didn't appreciate the values of the first and second generations. They basically assumed the good life would continue forever because it was all they had ever known.

I use the above story as an analogy of where I see the United States of America. I would say we are somewhere between the third and fourth generations.

Freedom and self-governance are not the norm in human history. In fact, most people who have lived on our planet through the ages have lived under some sort of tyranny, ruled by a pharaoh or a king or a sultan or a communist dictator or something similar. The Roman emperors had a centuries-long run, lording over 20% of the globe at the height of their rule.

Despite what modern historical revisionists would have us believe, America's founders did not invent slavery. It's been around for all of human history and is still in existence today. In fact, it was the ideas and writings of our founders that set in motion what eventually led to the end of slavery in our country. And it was hundreds of thousands of white soldiers who gave their lives in the Civil War so that black people would be free from slavery.

But I digress.

Many of our fellow Americans – especially the younger ones, say 30 and under – have little concept of how our country became the envy of the world: It all stems from our Christian roots. Without Christianity – in particular Protestantism – there would be no America. Christianity emphasizes the great value of the individual person in the eyes of God. That leads to a belief in human rights and freedom.

But our forefathers understood, as did subsequent generations, that without a reverence for Almighty God by a vast majority of her citizens, America would begin to crumble as the "sweet land of liberty." When you think that God is watching you and you are accountable to Him for your actions, you are far more likely to obey the law, live in peace, and care about your fellow man. If you lose that fear of God – as an individual or as a society (a nation) – it is certain that one way or another, you will crumble. You will die.

It's sad that many of our fellow Americans are ignorant of the truth of what I have written above – about the connection between Christianity and freedom. This ignorance is prevalent across our land and exists even inside our churches.

However, some Americans are not so much ignorant as they are defiant. They shake their fists at God and say they will do as they please with their lives, without regard for the consequences of living in rebellion against godly values.

Who knows if we can turn things around in our beloved country before it's too late? But we have to give it our all. Too much is at stake for our children, our grandchildren, and future generations.